D1561089

Elite • 160

World War II Infantry Assault Tactics

Gordon L Rottman • Illustrated by Peter Dennis

Consultant editor Martin Windrow

First published in Great Britain in 2008 by Osprey Publishing,
PO Box 883, Oxford, OX1 9PL, UK
PO Box 3985, New York, NY 10185-3985, USA
Email: info@ospreypublishing.com

A CIP catalogue record for this book is available from the British Library

ISBN: 978 1 84603 191 5

Editor: Martin Windrow
Page layout by Ken Vail Graphic Design, Cambridge, UK
Typeset in Helvetica Neue and ITC New Baskerville
Index by Alison Worthington
Originated by PPS Grasmere, Leeds, UK
Printed in China through World Print Ltd.

14 15 16 17 18   14 13 12 11 10 9 8 7 6 5

Osprey Publishing is part of the Osprey Group.

The Woodland Trust
Osprey Publishing is supporting the Woodland Trust, the UK's leading woodland conservation charity, by funding the dedication of trees.

www.ospreypublishing.com

Conversion factors:

Metric	English
200 grams (g)	7.5 ounces (oz)
300g	10.5oz
400g	14oz
500g	15.5oz
1 kilogram (kg)	2.2 pounds (lb)
1 centimetre (cm)	0.3937 inch (in)
1 metre (m)	3.2808 feet (ft)

TITLE PAGE **German photo from a sequence showing a pioneer squad making a training assault. In the final stages, they have breached the barbed wire and, screened by smoke grenades, divide around the sides of the enemy bunker. At left, one man carries slung on his back the single large tank of a *Flammenwerfer 35* flamethrower. The pale patches on the other men are slung bags for extra grenades. (Courtesy Concorde Publications)**

Acknowledgements

The author is indebted to Russell Butcher, Nik Cornish, Richard Pelvin, William Schneck, Akira Takizawa ('Taki'), James Tiffin, Ron Volstad and Martin Windrow for their assistance.

Artist's note

Glossary

alternate position   Position to be occupied when the first is compromised or untenable, covering the first position's field of fire.

assault (attack) position   Position from which the attack is launched.

assembly area   Position where units gather and prepare for the attack.

counter-attack   Attack mounted to dislodge or prevent the enemy from consolidating on a seized objective.

dead zone (dead ground)   Area that cannot be observed or covered by fire from a given position.

defilade   Position located so as to be protected from observation and fire.

enfilade   Fire that sweeps the length or long axis of a target.

field of observation/fire   Area that can be kept under surveillance and/or covered by fire from a particular position.

line of departure   Designated start line from which an assault is launched.

main line of resistance   The frontline trace of the main defensive positions.

main (primary) position   Principal position from which a weapon covers its sector of fire.

main (primary) attack   The most heavily weighted attack, intended to secure the main objective.

mutual support   Covering or supporting by fire from adjacent positions.

outpost   Position located forward of the main line of resistance, for security.

pillbox, bunker   Generic terms for fortified positions with overhead cover.

supplementary position   Position that covers with its fire an area other than the main area, e.g., to the flanks or rear.

sympathetic detonation   The simultaneous explosion of several adjacent unlinked charges in reaction to one being detonated.

WORLD WAR II INFANTRY ASSAULT TACTICS

INTRODUCTION

Every aspect of military planning, procurement and preparation, from the level of national governments downward, basically serves one single goal: to enable a platoon of riflemen to assault a clump of trees, a hillside, a pillbox or a city block. In the course of a single day in a major war hundreds of such 'insignificant' assaults occur, of which no two are exactly alike; and the sum total of their results makes the difference between an army's victory or failure.

Though they perform myriad other tasks, the close assault of an enemy-occupied objective is the central job of the rifle platoon – to 'close with and destroy or capture the enemy by fire and manoeuvre'. No matter how well equipped and trained beforehand, units had to be flexible enough to adapt their tactics and weapons employment to respond to the enemy's techniques, weapons, obstacles and fortifications (as well as to the terrain, vegetation and weather).

A British lance-corporal leading the Bren light machine gun (LMG) group within his infantry section (squad), winter 1944/45; by this date he has been issued a Sten 9mm sub-machine gun in place of a rifle – British infantry made more use of SMGs than their US counterparts. Advancing through thick woodland, the section are in line-abreast formation with the LMG group apparently on the left flank; they are alert, ready to deliver maximum firepower to the front at the moment of contact. Obviously, forested terrain greatly restricted the employment of supporting weapons, such as battalion machine guns and mortars, during an infantry assault. (Imperial War Museum B14413)

US infantry in action in the Normandy *bocage* near St Lô, 28 July 1944. Movement among these thick banked hedgerows was a lethal game of hide-and-seek with dug-in and concealed German defenders, and the GIs are well spaced out along the side of the lane. In this terrain infantry assaults over even short distances needed carefully planned supporting fire from machine guns, mortars and – if available – tanks. (NARA)

The most difficult assaults were those conducted against field fortifications – trench systems, bunkers, pillboxes, massive permanent fortifications, caves, tunnels or defended buildings – but attacks on any kind of objective had to deal with more than simply the objective itself. The assault platoon first had to make its way to and find the objective, often over rugged or overgrown terrain and at night and/or in bad weather. Man-made and natural obstacles had to be overcome. The attackers had to run a gauntlet of defensive fires, not just from the immediate defenders but also supporting fires from other directions. The assault might have to be launched straight out of the mouth of a landing craft or over the side of an amphibious tractor, after staggering out of a crash-landed glider, or after cutting oneself out of a parachute harness.

The rifle platoon

The rifle platoon was an all-purpose sub-unit, but it was the core of any assault. It seldom operated according to the table of organization, for three reasons: in combat, units were usually understrength; they might have more or fewer weapons than authorized; and they were task-organized for each mission. The standard organization was simply a basic structure allocating manpower and weapons, to be adapted in order to accomplish specific missions.[1]

The rifle platoon was the basic fire-and-manoeuvre sub-unit. Its two to four squads ('sections', 'groups' – in this text the US term squad is generally used for all, for the sake of brevity) did not attack independently; they operated as part of the platoon. A platoon operated in concert with another platoon of its company, with a third platoon in support — this 'two up and one back' scenario was almost universal. The support platoon might serve as a 'reserve' to reinforce success, but it might equally be sent to outflank the enemy or attack from another direction, to exploit an advantage, to maintain the tactical tempo by

---

[1] See Elite 105, *World War II Infantry Tactics: Squad and Platoon*

relieving an exhausted assault platoon, to protect an exposed flank, or to provide direct fire support to the assault platoons.

Combat engineers ('pioneers' or 'sappers') usually assisted in the construction of obstacles and minefields (though rifle platoons did much of the manual labour), the repair of roads and small bridges, and the building of protective bunkers for command posts and other critical facilities. However, engineer platoons often played a direct part in the assault, clearing routes through minefields, breaching or destroying obstacles, and attacking fortifications with demolitions and flamethrowers. In some armies standard doctrine called for the engineers to lead the infantry in the assault.

In all armies the **organization of rifle platoons** was surprisingly similar. The platoon headquarters consisted of a lieutenant, a platoon sergeant, and at least one enlisted man who might be a radio operator (though few World War II platoons had an organic radio), officer's orderly or message-runner. Two or three messengers might be assigned, more for liaison with company headquarters than with the squads; the platoon commander and sergeant could usually direct the squad leaders by voice, arm and hand signals and whistles. A medic might also be attached, but usually any immediate treatment had to be given by riflemen with additional medical training.

There was no 'weapons squad' within the platoon, but in some armies the platoon headquarters might have a single crew-served weapon – a light mortar or a shoulder-fired anti-tank (AT) weapon. The German platoon had a 5cm mortar until 1943, the British and Commonwealth platoon a 2in mortar, mainly for firing smoke and signal rounds. From 1943 Commonwealth platoons received a PIAT (projector, infantry, anti-tank), which replaced an AT rifle; the US added a bazooka to the platoon

15th (Scottish) Division at St Mauvieu, Normandy, during Operation 'Epsom' on 26 June 1944: in the cover of a banked hedge one of the three sections making up 12 Plat, B Coy, 6th Bn Royal Scots Fusiliers prepare to advance. Nine men are visible; centre, right of the Bren-gunner, the section leader is identified by his corporal's chevrons, Sten gun, and the machete on his hip. (IWM B5959)

in late 1943. Some Japanese platoons had a 5cm grenade-discharger section with three 'knee mortars', but these were often assigned downwards to the individual light machine gun (LMG)/rifle squads.

A platoon had three LMG/rifle squads (initially four, in the German and Soviet armies, but often in practice only three or even two due to casualties and personnel shortages, and the organization was soon reduced to three squads). Whether called a squad, section or group, these consisted officially of between 9 and 13 men, but often in combat of only 5 to 7, led by a corporal or junior sergeant. Each had a designated assistant leader; a light machine-gunner/automatic rifleman with an assistant/loader; an ammunition bearer, who doubled as a rifleman; and the rest were riflemen, at least one usually carrying a rifle-grenade launcher. Japanese sections sometimes had a 5cm 'knee mortar'; some Soviet sections had two LMGs, the platoon comprising two 'heavy' or two-gun sections and two 'light' one-gun sections.

Squads were usually divided into two groups or teams: a 2- to 4-man light machine gun group, and the rifle group. The squad leader might direct both rifle and LMG groups, lead the rifle group in person, or direct the fire of the LMG group. His assistant might lead the rifle group, control the LMG group, or simply position himself where he could best aid the control of the squad – including bringing up the rear to prevent straggling. The US squad began the war with a third team of two scouts, which the squad leader might accompany; this fell from use, as all riflemen are actually scouts, and the scout team often got pinned down if deployed forward.

The US Marine Corps had informally adopted a fire team concept, of 3 or 4 men centred on an automatic weapon, during the 1930s 'Banana Wars'. They did not accept the squad as the lowest manoeuvre element, and the USMC platoon began the war with three 9-man rifle squads, each with a Browning Automatic Rifle (BAR), plus a separate 8-man BAR squad with two weapons. In April 1943 they went to three 12-man squads each with two BARs capable of operating as two 6-man teams. In April 1944 they adopted a 13-man squad of a leader and three 4-man fire teams, each with a leader, a BAR man, his assistant and one rifleman.

Wider variety was seen in **company supporting weapons**. Most armies did not have a 'weapons platoon' in each company, but the US Army had a platoon with two MGs and three 60mm mortars, and the US Marines weapons platoon had three, later six MGs and three mortars. The Germans began the war with two tripod-mounted MGs and three AT rifles in separate sections, but these disappeared by 1942; the Soviets had a section of three 50mm mortars. Most infantry battalions had three rifle companies, but the British Commonwealth armies used four, and so (often) did the Japanese.

At **battalion** level, the US Army and Marines had a weapons company with six and four 81mm mortars, plus six and 12 heavy MGs, respectively. In 1944 the Marines transferred the MGs from battalion down to the rifle companies, and the mortars to the HQ company. The US Army battalion also had four 37mm anti-tank guns. The British and Commonwealth support company had six 3in mortars, six medium MGs, six 2pdr (later 6pdr) AT guns, plus assault pioneer and all-purpose light armoured carrier platoons. The Soviet battalion was the best armed (when weapons were available), with a company of nine heavy MGs, another of nine 82mm mortars, and a platoon of two 45mm AT guns plus some AT rifles. The German battalion had an MG company with 18 guns and six 8cm mortars. The Japanese battalion included an MG company with four, eight or 12 guns, plus an infantry gun platoon or company with two or four 7cm light guns, respectively.

At regimental (British Commonwealth, brigade) level the support weapons varied greatly, and might include AT guns, infantry guns (light howitzers) and heavy mortars. These weapons usually provided general rather than direct support for assault platoons.

THE OBJECTIVE

The 'objective' is the point or area that a unit is designated to seize, occupy or secure. During tactical planning, battalions were also assigned boundary lines – the corridor between adjacent units in which it operated and placed its fires; a unit could only fire into an adjacent unit's zone with permission, in order to prevent friendly fire casualties. Companies and platoons were seldom assigned boundaries; the sub-unit's span of control and the size of the area in which it operated were small enough to be controlled visually. Platoons were assigned objectives within the company's objective; and within that, depending on its nature and size, squads might also be assigned objectives – a certain section of a trench, a clump of brush, a specific bunker or building, or even one floor of a large building.

Composite diagram of a fully developed German defensive system, including the different types of obstacles and defensive positions liable to be encountered; depth, and mutually supporting positions, are the key features. In defence, the recommended frontages for a rifle platoon were 200–400 yards (US), 200–300 (British and Japanese), 250–300 (Soviet), and 200–450 yards (German). Frontages in the attack would be about half as wide.

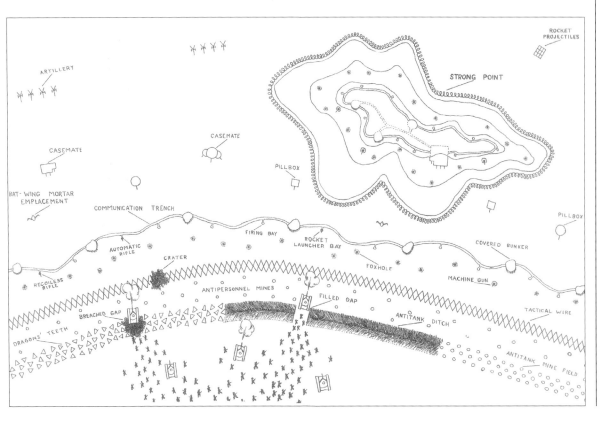

The base of fire for any infantry platoon dug in for defence was its squad LMGs. This Tommy is in a two-man slit trench at the base of a hedgerow, with overhead concealment added in the form of planks or an old door with a few inches of earth – this will give shelter from rain, but certainly not from mortar fire. A 12-magazine ammo chest has been dumped by his side, and he has three No.36 fragmentation grenades ('Mills bombs') ready to hand for last-ditch defence against a German rush. (Private collection)

DEFENSIVE TACTICS

At small-unit level there were few major national differences. The defending platoons, squads and supporting weapons occupied their assigned sectors, and covered their front, avenues of approach and exposed flanks with fire, interlocking with that of adjacent units to cover gaps between them. The appropriate weapons had to be sited to cover different avenues of approach for infantry and armour. This was complicated by the fact that the infantry would not attack across open ground in line formation (unless they had no other options), but used any available cover and concealment that might restrict observation and obstruct defensive fire.

The nature of the defensive position was affected by terrain and weather; by available materials, time and weapons; and by past experience. In a fortified area the nature of the fortifications, their dispersal and construction naturally governed the organization of a defence. Otherwise, given the same piece of ground to defend, no two platoons would be deployed in quite the same way; the defensive positions depicted in manuals of doctrine were simply the 'ideal' layout, on flat ground with clear fields of fire. In practice the frontage and depth of defensive positions were seldom so simple, owing to rough terrain, vegetation, under-manning, or reinforcement by crew-served weapons. Platoons were often forced to cover broader frontages because of tactical demands. The typical World War II three-regiment division, with three sub-units at each echelon, had two regiments on line and two battalions of each regiment up front, with two companies per battalion and two platoons per company on line; so, of the division's 81 rifle platoons, only 16 would be in the divisional front line, with eight others immediately supporting them.

Platoons normally deployed with all three squads on line. It was impractical for a 'reserve' squad to conduct a counter-attack within a platoon position, and little was achieved by using it to add depth to the defence; it was better to cover the platoon front with the maximum firepower. Early in the war, when the German platoon had a fourth rifle squad, this could be employed in defence to man outposts and conduct security patrols; after falling back it would occupy a position from which its fire could cover the rest of the platoon, or a gap between platoons. The Soviets did basically the same thing with their fourth squad, and did usually place it to the rear of the front line sections to give depth to the defence. The platoon commander positioned himself where he could see the greatest part of the platoon sector in order to control fire most effectively; his was more of an observation post than a command post.

Basic defensive principles included: covering the assigned frontage with fire by assigning each man and crew-served weapon a sector, ensuring if possible that the fires of more than one weapon overlapped; emplacing obstacles; establishing outposts and other security measures; co-ordinating fires with adjacent units and fire

German infantrymen practise drills on the Normandy coast before D-Day. Note the concrete anti-tank (AT) wall with slot-in steel I-beam barricade, and wire-wrapped 'knife-rest' or 'Spanish rider', all covered by an LMG – 'an obstacle not covered by fire is no obstacle'. If not posing for the photographer, the MG15 gunner would be emplaced further off and under better cover and concealment. (MHI)

support units; preparing alternate and supplementary positions; camouflaging, and continuously improving positions. At company and higher echelons depth in defence was critical, as were counter-attack plans and reserves to contain any breakthroughs. Defending units took measures to prevent surprise attacks, warn of the enemy's approach, and keep enemy patrols away from the main defensive positions, by means of reconnaissance patrols, outposts, observation posts in daytime and listening posts by night.

Early in the war doctrine usually prescribed that heavy weapons should engage the enemy at their maximum range, to disrupt his formations, slow his movement and inflict casualties as he advanced. However, it was found that long-range fire often had limited effect, wasted ammunition, and warned the enemy that they were nearing the main defences. Later, weapons would open fire simultaneously at optimum ranges depending on the terrain and fields of fire, usually within 300–500 yards – in effect, the attacker was ambushed. Of course, in dense forest and mountain terrain the engagement range was considerably shorter, sometimes just a few yards.

US troops push on through a breached roadblock in the *Westwall* or Siegfried Line on Germany's western frontier, passing I-beams cut by demolition charges, and concrete 'dragon's-teeth'.

Obstacles

Obstacles fell into two broad categories: anti-personnel, and anti-tank/anti-vehicle. (Beach/shore and underwater obstacles fell into a category of their own.)

The basic anti-personnel obstacle was barbed wire, which could be strung between stakes in multiple horizontal strands, in two or more parallel fences with connecting zig-zags between them; sloped diagonal strands could be staked to one or both sides, in single or double 'apron' fences to hamper an enemy attempting to cut or cross the barrier. Expanding 'concertina wire', typically in coils a yard in diameter, was spread either to reinforce other fences or as a barrier in its own right. Single strands were strung in low zig-zag patterns as tripwires or 'tanglefoot'. The 'Spanish rider' was a wire-wrapped portable wooden frame barrier (aka knife-rest, *cheval-de-frise*) useful for blocking roads, gullies and gaps in obstacles on a temporary basis.

Trees felled with the limbs toward the enemy – the ancient *abatis* – were effective against both personnel and vehicles. The even more ancient expedient of sharpened stakes driven in at an angle were reasonably easy to pull out by hand once they had been spotted, but could be effective if concealed in brush or high grass; bamboo *punji* stakes were widely used in the Pacific and South-East Asia theatres.

Anti-tank obstacles included AT ditches; concrete and stone AT walls and seawalls; rail or timber barricades; concrete 'dragon's-teeth' (truncated pyramids), tetrahedra (three-sided pyramids) and blocks set in rows; log and metal posts set vertically; steel hedgehogs (tripods of railway track or I-beams) and log hedgehogs (three-log tripods wrapped with barbed wire). Obstacles did not simply halt or slow attackers; properly sited, they could channel them into difficult terrain, minefields or pre-planned fire zones. Imaginatively sited and aligned at different angles, they could mislead attackers as to the location of the main line of defence. Sometimes they could be enhanced by concealing them to some degree; this was difficult, but placing them beneath trees, in brush and high grass, in gullies, on low ground or reverse slopes could mask them until attackers were almost upon them.

Among the most effective obstacles, especially to vehicles, are natural terrain features. While it is said that any terrain feature can be negotiated by troops, it can hamper their movement to the point that it is useless as an effective attack route. Swampland, soft snow, exceedingly muddy fields, flooded areas (including dammed streams) and flowing water obstacles, and dense vegetation could all frustrate organized infantry attacks, even if determined individuals or patrols might be able to overcome them. The same obstacles could halt AFVs, as could closely spaced and large-diameter trees, steep slopes, large rocks, railway and road embankments and cuttings, building rubble, bomb and shell craters and blown-down trees. The most effective obstacle system was one in which natural features were incorporated into the defensive plan, with man-made obstacles tied into the natural ones.

Mines were extensively employed, in numbers ranging from deep minefields thousands of yards broad to a few individual mines laid at a road junction. More armoured fighting vehicles (AFVs) were disabled by mines than by any other means; an AT mine could halt one simply by knocking off a track, or might destroy it entirely. Aerial bombs and artillery shells made particularly devastating mines if buried with pressure-activated fuses.

Anti-personnel mines were smaller but more sensitive, and mostly relied on blast effect to kill or maim soldiers. Since the blast of a buried mine was directed upward, and since soldiers were normally dispersed, it was usually a case of 'one mine, one man'; an infantry squad who simply rushed a minefield might well get through with only one or two casualties at worst. However, there were also fragmentation mines; these might be set above ground, or might incorporate an initial charge that threw them a yard or so into the air before detonation, thus taking out several soldiers. Some minefields were purely anti-personnel, but usually anti-personnel mines were laid among AT mines to hamper their clearance and kill infantry accompanying the tanks. Mines – especially AT types – might be booby-trapped to make their removal costly or at least time-consuming. The minefield 'owner' would place warning signs,

A stretch of the *Westwall*, showing the armoured MG cupola of a large, deeply buried concrete bunker, and a belt of concrete AT obstacles beyond. The bunkers were difficult to crack; sides, back and roof were covered with earth, and in addition to the MG mounted in the cupola the approaches were covered by open MG and other infantry positions. (NARA)

A Soviet sapper, wearing a camouflage coverall, works his way through barbed wire using large cutters. The forked stick visible above his left hand is for propping the cut ends out of his way; the small box in the foreground holds 200g TNT blocks, used to blast out the stakes when clearing a larger gap. Manual wire-cutting was useful when stealth was required; gripping the wire while cutting deadened the sound and prevented the ends springing back, so gloves were recommended. With two-man teams, one would grip the strand with both hands about 2in apart, and the other would use the cutters. If only one man was cutting, he could grip the strand with one hand about 2in from a stake and cut it next to the stake; a rag could be wrapped around the strand at the cut to help deaden the sound. (Courtesy Nik Cornish)

and possibly a barbed wire fence, on his side of the minefield. Dummy minefields were employed to delay and misdirect the enemy. Booby traps might also be encountered among any other type of obstacles; they were often made from hand grenades, small demolition charges or adapted mortar and artillery shells. While they caused difficulties and were nerve-wracking, according to US statistics only 2.9 per cent of the killed and 3.9 per cent of the wounded were caused by mines and booby traps.

No matter how well designed, constructed and sited an obstacle or minefield, it is worthless if not covered by observation and the fire of appropriate weapons. Machine guns covering a barbed wire belt will do little good when a tank crunches through it; artillery fire on a lengthy linear obstacle will be less than effective, since the lulls in the shelling and its uneven fall allow determined attackers to make breaches.

Field fortifications

Field fortifications are any temporary works built by troops for protection from fire and the weather – foxholes, trenches, bunkers, pillboxes, dug-outs and positions for crew-served weapons. Besides providing troop shelters, dug-outs housed command posts, observation posts, communications centres, aid stations, ammunition and supply points. The fortification of buildings – from a single farmhouse to a whole city block – was an art in itself, and could produce stubborn redoubts. Permanent reinforced concrete fortifications were mainly for protecting artillery and AT weapons, but usually included some firing positions for infantrymen, machine guns and other light weapons. To reinforce the defence of fixed fortifications, infantry field works were emplaced around and among them. US troops attacking the *Westwall* (Siegfried Line) also credited dug-in German tanks and self-propelled guns (SPGs) with an efficiency rating of 40 per cent, and considered them much more troublesome than bunkers.

In some ways permanent fortifications were a liability to the defender: while they offered protection from shells and bombs, they were fairly easy to locate, and they tended to induce among their defenders a false sense of security and a loss of initiative. They offered only limited fields of fire in fixed directions, resulting in blind spots that required supplementary fighting positions to be dug in order to provide all-round defensive fires. Any type of field fortification had to be well sited to cover its sector of fire and enemy avenues of approach, but the only thing that made it worthwhile was its integration into an overall defence plan of mutually supporting fires – a single pillbox not protected by other positions was worthless. What made attacking fortified positions so costly in infantrymen's lives was that each position was covered by others to its flanks and rear, and each of those by yet further positions. Another consideration in siting a position was to place it on terrain that was difficult to cross by foot or AFV; the Japanese learned and applied this lesson well.

Camouflage, from the ground and the air, was critical. Efforts were made to conceal the position so well that it would not be detected until it opened fire; even then, ideally, it would be difficult to see clearly among terrain features, vegetation, and the smoke and dust of battle, owing to its weapons' smokeless propellant and flash suppression. Even when a position was detected, camouflage could hide its exact nature. Embrasures (firing ports) were kept small, though this was a trade-off between concealment and effective fields of fire. Entrances were usually sited in the rear or side, protected by a trench and covered by a firing port or another position.

The use of decoy positions could cause attackers to judge a sector as more heavily defended than it was, deceiving them into redirecting their assault into a genuinely strongly defended zone (which careful camouflage could make appear the weaker). At the very least, dummy positions could make the enemy waste ammunition; and attacking infantry might fire on them or even attack them, thus exposing themselves to fire from actual positions.

A common type of AT ditch, with a trapezoidal profile. This one, in unstable soil, is shored up with tree branches packed down behind retaining posts to prevent erosion; such revetting also hampered efforts to blast in the walls to create crossing ramps. Attackers were seldom surprised by AT ditches, which were easily detectable by aerial or ground reconnaissance.

BREACHING OBSTACLES

There are three ways to surmount or defeat an obstacle: go around it, go over it, or go through it. Bypassing an obstacle is ideal, but may not be possible; but if it cannot be avoided, then it can be breached. Breaching any but a massively robust obstacle is a relatively simple matter provided that it is not covered by fire (though it usually is). Armies were well prepared for such tasks; since World War I new techniques had been developed, infantry and engineer training included obstacle-breaching as a basic skill, and the appropriate tools and materials were routinely carried.

There were two levels of breaching: hasty, and deliberate. Hasty methods allowed little if any reconnaissance, planning or preparation; the tactical situation was such that the obstacle had to be breached immediately and with the resources at hand – which could be costly in lives and material. In deliberate breaching, obstacles were reconnoitred and plotted thoroughly, forces were tasked to breach them, and the necessary tools and materials were provided.

The means ranged from the crude (wrenching obstacles out by hand, climbing over or cutting through them), to the sophisticated (blasting with demolitions, or employing special assault vehicles

British infantry cross some kind of wet obstacle on a hasty footbridge of timbers put in place by 15th (Scottish) Div engineers. The dumped lumber in the background suggests that a more substantial crossing will soon be built. (Private collection)

that destroyed them by brute force). Ditches, gullies, streams and trenches could be crossed by bridging or filling the gap. 'Forcing through' an obstacle or minefield could be costly, and the attrition of tanks and troops had to be weighed against the expected tactical gain. Regardless of the breaching method used or the type of obstacle, the assault force almost invariably faced direct and indirect fire from the objective and adjacent positions; this influenced the means and weapons employed, the supporting fires, routes, and unit organization.

Anti-personnel obstacles

During World War II **barbed wire** as dense at that employed in World War I was seldom encountered – which was fortunate, since in this case breaching methods had not improved much. Tanks could crush wire and a bulldozer could plough through it; but few armies had armoured dozers or dozer blades to mount on tanks, and deep wire could easily tangle in a tank's running gear, halting it as effectively as a mine. Occasionally tanks dragged out entire sections of wire entanglements with a tow cable; but suitable AFVs were not always available, and might not be able to approach the barriers because of terrain, mines or covering AT weapons.

The preferred method of breaching wire was **demolitions**. Attaching individual charges to stakes was too time-consuming and difficult, and simply throwing in large satchel charges was only marginally effective. To destroy dense barriers with artillery and heavy mortars required the infantry to be pulled well back for safety, a high degree of accuracy, and heavy expenditure of ammunition that could be better spent on higher-value targets. Artillery also created craters and a tangle of chopped-up wire and uprooted stakes that were still difficult for infantry to negotiate.

The 'bangalore torpedo' was the wire-breaching charge of choice; typically, these were light-gauge steel tubes 4ft–6ft long and 1¼in–2in in diameter, filled with 1½lb–2lb of explosive per foot of length. A number of tubes could be linked together end-to-end into a string by means of locking collars, and a snap-on nosecone on the front torpedo prevented it from snagging on the wire as it was pushed in. A detonator well was provided in the end of each tube, and a detonator assembly was inserted in the rear torpedo of the string. The string was pushed into the wire, the number depending on the depth of the barrier – a maximum 200ft on favourable ground, 100ft on rough. For particularly dense entanglements two or more strings could be shoved through side-by-side.

Field-expedient bangalores were made by packing steel pipe, drainpipe or lengths of bamboo with explosives. Another expedient form was made by attaching demolition blocks to a plank, several inches apart, inserting a detonating system in the last charge and relying on sympathetic detonation to set them all off together.

Manual cutting through wire was the most frequent means of hasty breaching. Armies issued 8in- to 14in-long wire-cutters to squads, and a man could typically cut a yard-wide gap through 3 yards depth of entanglement in one minute. Units also had larger (18in–24in) cutters, which could also cut padlocks and cable.

Going over the wire was another option. Blankets, overcoats, 'liberated' quilts or bits of carpet, canvas or wire mesh rolls could be thrown over the barrier, and scaling-ladders or even logs could also be used as bridges. One oft-practiced method was for one soldier to throw his body across a narrow barrier, holding his rifle vertically in front of him for a degree of protection, and allow others to run over this human bridge. While this dramatic drill could work, the hero needed help to extricate himself from the wire afterwards, which rather reduced the time-saving benefit.

Anti-personnel obstacles other than wire had to be dealt with pragmatically. Craters and all kinds of rubble and debris significantly hampered foot troops; on some Pacific islands the Marines encountered such gouged and blasted terrain and so much scattered wreckage that it severely delayed the advance even of their AFVs. The same applied in heavily bombed and shelled urban areas – such as, notoriously, Cassino town in 1943–44.

Anti-tank obstacles

By definition, AT obstacles were massive, robust and tough to breach; but to be effective they had to be covered by fire – not just AT but anti-infantry weapons, to ward off either breaching parties or infiltrators seeking out the covering AT weapons beyond. They were often in exposed locations, since tanks needed relatively open terrain; this denied cover and concealment to breaching parties.

Without aids a soldier can climb a 6ft wall; an 8ft–10ft wall can be surmounted by other men standing close and boosting their comrades up, before they themselves are pulled up. The task is made easier by scaling-ladders or knotted ropes with grappling hooks, but these were not available at short notice to ordinary line infantry platoons. British Commandos and US Rangers had such aids for long-planned operations; and they (and paratroopers) often carried toggle ropes – a 4ft–6ft length of ½in rope, with a loop spliced in one end and a wooden T-handle in the other. These could be linked end-to-end and used to climb obstacles, or even to make rope bridges across gaps.

'Dragon's-teeth' AT obstacles were linked together by concrete foundations, to prevent them simply being overturned and dragged out of the way individually.

The massive obstacles themselves offered cover, but they were ranged by MGs and mortars and often sprinkled with wire, anti-personnel mines and booby traps, making them extremely dangerous to breaching parties.

Once reached, AT obstacles had to be destroyed, not simply gapped; this required large demolition charges – sometimes entire crates – and shaped-charge munitions of different types. Above-ground linear obstacles such as hedgehogs, posts, dragon's-teeth and rocks required large charges to be fitted to each and detonated simultaneously; it was hoped that any remaining mines and booby traps would be sympathetically detonated by this shattering blast. Rubble and debris then had to be removed before the gap could be used. Less robust obstacles might be dismantled using pry bars, pick-mattocks, sledge hammers and axes. Bulldozers or tracked AFVs might be able to push or pull obstacles out of the way, but this was not always easy. The Germans often chained hedgehogs together; dragon's-teeth were linked by concrete footings, creating a single large unit. One solution was for a dozer to mound earth up over the teeth, making an elevated roadway for AFVs.

Vertically embedded logs, rails, and concrete or stone blocks were also hard to displace, and concrete and stone AT walls and seawalls were especially difficult to breach; massively constructed, these required hundreds of pounds of explosives. Again, if they were not too high, earth ramps could be bulldozed up to surmount them. If the wall was backfilled (i.e. earth-filled behind the wall to its full height), cratering charges placed just behind it would collapse it outwards, thus creating a ramp of sorts. Walls could also be breached by mounting large shaped charges against the face, suspended from poles leaning against the wall.

Crossing gaps

Streams, gullies, drainage and irrigation ditches, canals and AT ditches posed special difficulties for attackers and demanded a considerable effort to cross. Portable bridges might be emplaced by engineers, but these had to be able to support a tank weighing many tons. Such a bridge was not easily portable, and if the gap was wide, a central support was needed; the edge of the ditch also had to be stable enough to support the weight of the bridge and the AFV crossing it, so to prevent the edges collapsing the bridge had to be somewhat longer than the gap's width. Any form of bridging was time-consuming, and exposed engineers to fire; portable bridges delivered by AFVs were in their infancy and rarely available.

Another means to cross a gap was to fill it, at least to the width of an AFV; large demolition charges could be placed just behind the edges on both sides to blow down the banks. This might not be sufficient to fill a deep gap, and ramps might have to be bulldozed into both sides and the soil used as bottom fill. These methods required earth-moving equipment, and could not be employed in deep gaps or those carrying flowing water. A more portable means, dating back to the Romans, was the fascine – a lashed bundle of logs or brushwood – of which numbers could be dumped into gaps; the British made extensive use of these.

Tanks can generally cross a gap only about one-third their ground-contact length or less. Anti-tank ditches were constructed in great numbers, sometimes running for thousands of yards, sometimes simply defending small strongpoints, and sometimes dug in overlapping multiples. In cross-section they might be rectangular, triangular or trapezoidal, and of very varied dimensions. On the uphill side of slopes, if a shelf was cut with a vertical back wall even of comparatively low height, this could greatly hamper a tank's crossing ability, and spoil was often thrown to the attacker's side to increase the effectiveness of a ditch. To counter the cover they provided to attacking infantry AT ditches might be mined or booby-trapped, filled with wire, stakes,

British Sherman IIC Firefly tank crossing a drainage channel in Italy on an Ark folding bridge; this three-section, 45ft bridge was mounted on an M4 tank hull which was simply driven down into the ditch. Note the fascine bundle lashed to the Firefly's bow. The British made extensive use of these, including large ones made of logs and secured by cable or chain; lengths of pipe might even be incorporated, to serve as culverts when there was flowing water in the ditch that was to be filled.

Soviet sappers search for mines, using a probe on a long pole and a VIM mine-detector; both are armed with PPSh-41 SMGs. The prober is checking along a street kerb – the Germans were imaginative in their placement of mines.

In North Africa, British engineers developed an effective organization for minefield-breaching. The platoon was led by a reconnaissance party, flanked by escorts with Thompson guns. They were followed at intervals by 'bangalore men', then tape-layers, and the officer in command. Next came two-man teams with electronic mine-detectors (three teams, for an 8-yard lane); then mine-markers; then mine-lifters, with the platoon sergeant bringing up the rear. Last of all came lane-markers to fit signs and lamps along the outer edges of the cleared lane. (Courtesy Nik Cornish)

tangled branches and brush, or flooded. Occasionally infantry positions were sited to enfilade their length, and they were routinely registered by artillery and mortars.

When attacking across AT ditches and other gaps the infantry would usually cross first to clear the far side of defenders, while engineers used some hasty means to get AFVs across to support the assault. Once the far side was secured the engineers cleared any mines and installed more substantial and numerous crossings.

Minefields

Ideally mines were laid in dense patterns, buried, well camouflaged and booby-trapped. In practice the time- and labour-intensive process of laying them meant that they were often poorly camouflaged, or even left exposed. This made life easier (and longer) for clearance parties; they were still capable of stopping AFVs, but visually detected AT mines could be exploded or disabled by accurate MG fire. Anti-personnel mines had to be buried to be of any use, but in sand-desert mines sometimes became exposed by the wind. Mines were laid in multiple rows at prescribed intervals; this allowed clearance engineers to locate them more easily once the pattern was discerned.

The first step in breaching a minefield was to locate it. Engineers looked for discoloured and disturbed soil, displaced or wilted vegetation, subsidence depressions, tripwires, footprints made by mine-laying parties, and dead livestock. Incompetent mine-layers might even

leave dumps of discarded shipping crates, packing materials and arming pins, thus revealing the types of mine and even if some were booby-trapped. Besides visual means, probing was the most common hasty detection method; although slow and unnerving, it is actually not all that dangerous for an experienced man. Probing at an angle was done with a bayonet (by hand or on a rifle), a short sharpened stick, or a longer pole fitted with a thin spike; the British entrenching tool handle had a fitment taking the No.4 spike bayonet for use in this way.

Electronic mine detectors registered the presence of buried metallic objects by magnetic response – which meant that they also detected dud shells and fragments, old tin cans, and any other kind of discarded or scrap metal. They could not be used along railway tracks; and some countries employed wooden box, ceramic and glass mine casings that were undetectable by electronic means.

Strings of bangalore torpedoes could be pushed into anti-personnel minefields and detonated to blast a narrow gap; but such a gap still had to be probed, as mines might have survived, and sensitized mines might be on the edges. Tripwire-activated mines could be detonated by throwing a grappling hook across and dragging the rope back from under cover. Tracked AFVs were driven through anti-personnel minefields with the infantry gingerly following in the tracks, far enough to the rear to avoid fragments (and fire ricocheting off the tank). More blatant means were used on occasion: infantry simply charged across regardless of the cost, or herded livestock in front of them. In non-Western armies men from penal units were sometimes marched through minefields, and there were instances in the Philippines and China of the the Japanese forcing civilians across.

US combat engineers, one carrying an SCR-625 mine-detector, pass others de-mining a roadside at La Haye du Puits, Normandy, on 11 July 1944. Note the platter-shaped German *Tellerminen* AT mines (*Teller* means platter) already lifted and placed on the wall. Much more dangerous to infantry was the 'bouncing bitch' or 'castrator' – the *Schrapnellminen 35* or *44* bounding anti-personnel mine, called the 'S-mine' by the Allies. Buried with only the fuse exposed and connected to a tripwire, it was difficult to detect among brush and grass; when tripped, an initial charge sent it 3ft–5ft into the air before it detonated, spraying 360 steel ball bearings in all directions. (NARA)

19

A lane at least a yard wide was cleared for troops, although a two-yard gap was preferred for two-way traffic and to accommodate wheeled crew-served weapons and stretcher (litter) parties; vehicle lanes for one-way traffic were a minimum of 4 yards wide. Regardless of the breaching means, the gap's entry and exit and the lane itself were clearly marked in some manner. Engineers would mark the near edge, and either mark the far edge or retain the enemy markers. The signs used depended on nationality, but white and/or red signs with black letters and arrows were common; the Germans, at least, also used the death's-head sign beloved of folklore. Flags, cloth strips and tape were also used; specific signs warned of mines, booby traps and unexploded munitions; and at night lamps, reflectors and fire-pots were employed.

DEMOLITION MATERIALS

General description

For obvious reasons of space only the most commonly used materials, and a selection from the large numbers of charges and related items, are described here.

Basic **demolition charges** were available in cylindrical (cartridge) or rectangular (slab, block) shapes; they varied from fist-size, to a charge requiring two men to emplace it and fitted with carrying handles. Smaller charges were protected by paper or cardboard, larger ones by thin metal covers, all pierced by one or more threaded detonator wells; plastic explosives (PE) did not need wells, since a hole was made simply with a spike. Most countries had a standard threading for detonators and other firing devices, making them interchangeable between different munitions (including mines and grenades, allowing them to be set up as booby traps). There were also special munitions including shaped and cratering charges, ring charges for cutting gun barrels, and bangalore torpedoes (see above).

Shaped or hollow charges are more usually associated with AT munitions, but larger types were extensively used to attack fortifications and breach walls; they often enabled infantry and engineers to defeat with hand-delivered munitions even massive fortifications that had previously been resistant to heavy artillery. Hand-emplaced shaped charges, ranging from cup-size to 50kg (110lb), were used to penetrate reinforced concrete walls, steel doors, embrasure shutters and gun cupolas.

TNT was among the most commonly used **military explosives** and was a component of others. The relative effectiveness of military explosives is rated by their blast effect compared to TNT, which has an effectiveness value of '1'. PETN has a value of 1.42, but is too sensitive to shock and flash for military use. Compounds including amatol (1.20), tetrytol (1.22), and pentolite (1.26) were powerful but stable explosives; these were widely employed for combat demolitions, and pentolite (TNT plus PETN) was used in many shaped charges owing to its high detonating velocity.

One of the first military explosives was picric acid, widely used by the Japanese and Germans. It had the same effectiveness rating as TNT, but reacted to metals to create dangerously sensitive compounds, so the inside of projectiles had to be varnished. The British also still made use of an early explosive, guncotton – compressed cotton blocks dipped in nitric and sulphuric acids; very unstable, it was stored wet in sealed containers. Blasting dynamite was little used in actual combat, since it was sensitive to gunfire and to temperature extremes. Plastic explosives were in their infancy in World War II; they were composed of RDX or Hexogen – explosives more powerful than TNT – mixed with plasticizing materials to form a mouldable compound. Early plastic explosives were often oily, had a strong odour, generated unsafe fumes, and became stiff or crumbly at low or high temperatures.

Many accessories and devices were used in conjunction with explosives, but some were basic. **Safety fuse** (aka time, delay, Bickford fuse) is about ⅛in in diameter and consists of a uniform-burning pyrotechnic compound core within a tight, spirally wrapped fibre sheath, and an outer treated-fabric waterproof cover (in fact, often susceptible to moisture). The burning rate of any safety fuse depends on the country of manufacture and the manufacturing lot, and must be checked for each spool before its use.

Detonating cord or instantaneous fuse

(aka detcord or primacord in US slang, cordex in British) was commonly used to link charges for simultaneous detonation. Usually of ⅛in diameter and covered with plastic or treated-fabric waterproofing, the cord is filled with a high-velocity explosive, usually PETN, that detonates at a speed of 21,000ft per second – i.e. something in the order of 200 miles per minute; it is an explosive charge in its own right. To detonate it, either a non-electric blasting cap was taped to the end and a length of safety fuse inserted in the cap, or an electric blasting cap or some form of mechanical firing device was attached. The detcord could be inserted in the fuse wells of demolition charges, with a blasting cap crimped to the end to ensure detonation of the main charge. If several wraps of detcord were turned around the blocks to link any number of charges, it detonated all connected charges instantaneously.

While all sorts of **detonators**, igniters and boosters were used to explode demolitions, the No.8 detonator was the most common. This was nothing more than the international standard commercial No.8 non-electric blasting cap: a thin-walled aluminium or copper tube 2½in long × ¼in diameter, partly filled with PETN, and topped with a small, highly sensitive initiator of fulminated mercury, potassium chlorate and antimony sulphite. One end of the tube is open to accept a length of safety fuse or detcord, crimped in place. Electric blasting caps required

American 22lb satchel charges have been stacked against an AT wall, and the instructor demonstrates how the free ends of each satchel's detcords are linked together by square knots. Extremely heavy demolition charges were necessary to blast a way through AT seawalls facing beaches. One experiment involved stacking 46x 22lb TNT satchel charges in two rows in a wooden rack almost the entire width of the blade of a tank-dozer. The idea was that the tank would lower the blade and leave the rack tipped against the wall; the charges were linked with detcord, so all 920lb of TNT could be detonated simultaneously.

the skills of a well-trained specialist using either a battery or a blasting machine to detonate them via a firing wire. They were little used for assault demolitions, due to the danger of their being set off by static electricity (or nearby lightning discharges).

Small demolition charges might be secured to the target object, but more often bundles of charges in haversacks, sandbags or simply wrapped in canvas were used as '**satchel charges**'. These could be secured to obstacles, or simply thrown into pillboxes or caves to destroy the occupants. When charges were fastened to obstacles they were usually linked together by detcord, either in a line-main or ring-main. A length of detcord with a blasting cap on one end was inserted in each charge's fuse well; the other end was knotted to a length of detcord running in a line or circle, connecting all the charges. The line-main or ring-main had a 'standard firing device' attached: a length of safety fuse of the desired delay time, with a blasting cap on one end and a friction fuse igniter on the other (this same firing device was used to detonate individual charges or satchel charges). A delay of 7 seconds or so was used when throwing charges into targets, and a longer one when attached to obstacles to allow the firer to escape. To ensure detonation, two standard firing devices were often fitted to a charge.

A '**pole charge**' was basically a satchel charge or wired-together bundle of charges fitted to a long pole. This allowed the soldier to reach over wire, rubble or burning flamethrower fuel and to jam it into a bunker embrasure without exposing himself in front of the firing port. The pole also made it awkward for the occupants to throw it out in time. An infantryman on foot could also place the charge on a tank's vulnerable top plates. In house-to-house fighting demolitions were used to blast openings through building walls to gain entry, as well as openings between rooms. It was during the December 1943 battle for Ortona, Italy, that Canadians perfected the '**mouse-holing charge**' (see Plate F) invented for the British Home Guard.

Within enclosed structures blast effect is greatly magnified, and it is reflected from hard surfaces. **Injuries** resulting from blast over-pressure (concussion) and explosive flash include lacerations, internal injuries, damage to eyes and eardrums, burns on exposed skin, and actual dismemberment. The extent of injuries depends on proximity to the explosion and, if in an enclosed space, the size of that space. Fragments (aka splinters, shrapnel) are the real killers, however. A grenade body, shattered by the detonation of its explosive filler, produces scores of fragments; the more fragments, the more casualties – and of greater severity, due to multiple wounds – but the most important factor is fragment size. If they are too small they may inflict only troublesome but not incapacitating wounds. Some fragments may be too light to travel out to an effective casualty radius; or they may lack sufficient mass and velocity (3,000-plus feet per second is considered necessary) to penetrate thick layers of winter clothing, or go deep enough into the body to damage organs and arteries. However, secondary fragmentation – e.g. gravel, stone and wood splinters, pieces of concrete and brick or glass shards – can also be deadly.

National specifics: United States

(Note that some additional details of Allied and Axis items are given in the commentaries to Plates C, D and E.)

Detcord was yellowish-green, waterproof, and detonated at 20,000ft per second. Time fuse was bright green and burned at a rate of 1ft in 30–45 seconds. The worldwide standard No.8 blasting cap was used.

A time delay fuse might be ignited to allow the demolition men to withdraw, or the bangalore might be detonated electrically. The ground reflected the blast upwards, shredding the wire and blowing a gap at least a yard wide. (One danger was accidentaly setting off a mine while the tubes were being shoved through the entanglement, since the torpedoes would also detonate.) The explosion of a bangalore created a good deal of fragmentation from the tube, barbed wire and stakes.

23

German 100g *Bohrpatrone 28* charge ('1928 boring cartridge') – here dated 1941 – packed in tan compressed paper between Bakelite ends. The detonator well is sealed with a pink disc to identify TNT filler. (Private collection)

Early basic demolition charges were yellow with black and red markings for high visibility. In 1942 olive drab packaging with yellow markings was introduced (though ¼lb TNT charges continued to be made with yellow packaging – Plate C5 & C6). The metal end caps on some charges were black or sometimes tinned. Non-explosive items were OD with black markings. Before America's entry into the war small nitrostrach blocks were the standard demolitions. The ¼lb charge (measuring 1¼in × 1¼in × 1¼in) was composed of three blocks wrapped in wax paper, with a cap hole extending right through the charge. Four ¼lb charges were packaged and used in a 1lb pack, 2⅜in to a side; four circles on the sides were aligned with the cap holes at both ends of the ¼lb blocks. The ½lb charge (1in × 1in × 3⁵⁄₁₆in) was packed in cardboard with tin end caps, and a cap hole at one end. In 1940 nitrostrach was replaced by ½lb TNT blocks in unchanged packaging; a 1lb TNT charge in OD wrapping was introduced in 1943.

The tetrytol M1 chain demolition charge was an assembly of eight asphalt-impregnated, paper-covered 2½lb blocks cast on to 15ft 4in of detcord, with an 8in space between each block and 24in at either end; a tetryl booster was embedded in both ends. The M2 charge was the same except for lacking the detcord link. Both charges were packed eight to an OD canvas haversack weighing 22lbs — the 'satchel charge' (Plate C4).

The first US plastic explosive was Composition C; this came in ½lb (1in × 1½in × 6in) and 2½lb (2in × 2in × 11in) blocks wrapped in white and OD glazed paper respectively, and packed in cardboard cartons. Eight of the larger charges were issued in a haversack. They saw less use than the 2½lb M3 (see Plate C7) and ½lb M4 (2in × 1½in × 6in) charges of improved C2, in OD wrapping and packaged the same as the Comp C.

The Navy used the Mk 20 charge or 'Hagensen pack'; this was 2lb of C2 (1½in × 2½in × 12in) encased in a canvas cover with 5ft of detcord folded inside when the charge was moulded, and 6ft looped and stowed on the outside; 5ft of securing cord with a flat steel hook was stowed on the other side. The Navy Mk 23 charge was 2½lb of TNT (2in × 2in × 11in) with a single pentolite booster cast inside, eight blocks being strung on detcord in a similar manner to the M1 chain demolition charge.

Special charges included the 13lb M1 bangalore torpedo (Plate C1). The M1 shaped charge had a sheet metal body with three folding steel legs; the M2 had a fibreboard body with a fibreboard collar the same length as the M1's legs, for stand-off (Plate C2). Both weighed 13lb including 10lb of pentolite; the M1 could cut a 1½in-diameter hole through 8in of armour plate, or a 2⅜in diameter hole through 30in of reinforced concrete. A second charge placed directly over the first hole would cut a 45in-deep hole and enlarge the diameter to about 3in at the surface and 2in at the bottom. The 15lb M2A3 was similar but had 11½lb of pentolite. The 45lb M3 shaped charge (Plate C3) held 30lb of pentolite; it had a three-leg stand that clamped around the base for a 15in stand-off, and could punch a 60in deep hole through concrete. The 43lb cratering charge (8¼in diam × 17in) held 40lb of ammonium nitrate; it was designed for cratering roads and runways, destroying bridges, and other demolition tasks requiring bulk charges. It was packed in a waterproof metal cylinder with a cap well and a detcord tunnel on the side.

British Commonwealth

British No.11 safety fuse was black, and burned at about 1 yard in 20 seconds. 'Instantaneous fuse' was orange or red, and burned at 90ft per second. British 'cordex' or 'instantaneous detonating fuse' was encased in flexible lead- or aluminium-coloured composition. To ensure positive detonation the British used a 1oz Mk II dry guncotton primer with a blasting cap crimped to a length of safety fuse (Plate D7); this assembly was known as a 'demolition set'. Ten primers were packed in a black metal tube sealed by a screw cap. Standard blasting caps were the No.8 Mk I and No.27 Mk I.

A variety of small basic demolition charges – cartridges or slabs – usually came in buff packaging. The 4oz ammonal cartridge (1in diam × 5in) was wrapped in black rubberized fabric; the 1lb wet guncotton slab (1⅜in × 2¼in × 6in) came in a tin container; and the 1¼lb TNT slab (1½in × 3in × 6in) was wrapped in buff paper. From 1942 cream-coloured PE began replacing guncotton, ammonal and TNT. The ¼lb 'gelidnite' cartridge was wrapped in waxed paper, and one of improved PE in cellophane; the ½lb PE No.2 charge was paper-wrapped (Plates D1 & D2).

Among special charges, the No.1 Mk I was a small, hand-emplaced shaped charge for penetrating armour, concrete and masonry, fielded in early 1942; this 'beehive' charge (Plate D6) had a cylindrical stand-off collar and three 4⅝in stamped-metal legs riveted on for additional stand-off. Weighing about 8lb, with a 6¾lb pentolite or RDX/TNT filling, and a fuse well in the top, it could punch a 2⅛in-diameter hole through 2⅛ft of concrete. The 27¼lb No.3 Mk I Hayrick demolition charge (Plate D5) contained 15lb of pentolite or RDX/TNT inside a satchel-like metal container; this was a linear-shaped charge used for cutting beams. The 25lb Mk I and II bangalore torpedoes were 62½in long. The above charges were usually painted 'service brown', a chocolate shade, with white markings, and a red band indicating that they were filled with high explosives. A green-black-green band further identified the filler as pentolite, and yellow-blue-yellow as RDX/TNT.

The No.73 Mk I AT 'hand percussion grenade' was more commonly called the 'thermos flask', from its cylindrical shape and screw-on plastic safety cap (Plate D3). First issued in late 1940, it could only be thrown 10–15 yards, and could blow off a tank track. In practice it was more commonly used for demolitions after removing the impact fuse assembly; withdrawn from service in late 1941, it was reissued for that purpose in early 1943. Weighing 4¼lb, it was filled with 3¼lb of polar ammonal gelatin dynamite or nitrogelatin – both very susceptible to open flames and to impact detonation by small-arms fire.

The No.75 AT grenade/mine or 'Hawkins grenade', introduced in 1942, was a versatile munition that could be buried as a mine, thrown as an AT grenade, or used as a demolition charge (Plate D4). Weighing 2¼lb, it was a rectangular tin can with rounded side edges, and held 18oz of ammonal or TNT. It was fitted with a pressure plate on one side, and with holders for blasting caps and delay fuse or cordex. The US M7 light AT mine/grenade was developed from the 'Hawkins' in 1943.

German 1kg *Sprengbüchse 24* ('1924 demolition petard') – here dated 1940 – in its dark green zinc case. The three detonator wells are sealed with yellow discs to identify picric acid filler. (Private collection)

Soviet Union

Several models of detcord, coloured red, were used: DSh-31 and -34 (5100m/sec), DSh-36 and -40 (7600m/sec), DSh-39 (6500m/sec), and DSh-43 (6500m/sec – the only type that could be used underwater). Time delay fuse was grey, and burned at 1cm per second.

Demolition charges were similar to German patterns, but the Red Army made no use of portable shaped-charge munitions. Paper-wrapped TNT charges came in three sizes: 75g cartridges, 200g blocks, and 400g blocks (Plates D11–13). The latter two were also found filled with picric acid *(melinit)*. All had a cap well in the end, while the 400g size had a second in the side. Charges of 500g weight were also procured from France (with Russian markings), in various blends of TNT and lower-powered ammonium nitrate/xylite. These charges were yellow with black markings, but tan or buff waxed paper was also used. TNT unitary charges encased in metal containers, similar to those used by the Germans, saw some use; they were painted green drab and issued in 1kg, 3kg, 5kg and 10kg sizes. Dimensions are not available, but they were similar in size to their German counterparts (see below).

Bangalore torpedoes – which the Russians called 'hose charges' – were issued in 1m (5.1kg) and 2m (11kg) lengths, and were 52mm in diameter; the TNT filler was only about half the weight of the complete charge. These were scarce, so expedient hose charges were made from any available piping.

For heavy blast charges the required number of blocks were simply wrapped up in canvas tied with wire or string, with a blasting cap and delay fuse inserted. Another method was to wire pairs of 400g blocks on opposite sides at both ends of a 0.75m-long plank, wrap and tie the assembly in canvas, and insert a cap and delay fuse; the result – looking something like a barbell with rectangular weights at the ends – was thrown into embrasures, where its length made it difficult to throw out.

Much use was made of captured German demolition materials. So many of the *Haft-Hohlladung 3kg* (AT magnetic hollow charge – see below) were captured that it became almost a standard item.

Germany

The standard blasting cap igniter assembly *(Sprengkapselzünder)* consisted of a pull friction-igniter *(Brennzünde – BZ 29)*; 1m or 2m of time fuse *(Zeitzündschnur)*, cut to the desired length and re-crimped; a detonator holder *(Zünderhälter)* in Bakelite – a hard, plastic-like synthetic resin that

British Royal Engineers sergeant displaying a captured German 12.5kg *Hohlladung* ('hollow charge'), measuring 11in in diameter by 8.1in high. The dark green sheet metal casing has a detonator well and a web carrying handle at the top. Lacking any 'stand-off' effect, this pre-war munition was soon replaced by the more powerful 13.5kg type with folding legs at the base. (Private collection) does not conduct electricity; and a blasting cap *(Sprengkapsel Nr.8 A1)*. Time delay fuse was black or grey, and burned at 1cm per second or slower. Detcord *(Knallzündschnur)* was light green. Electric igniter devices included the *Glühzündapparat 26, 37*, and *39*.

The Germans used TNT or picric acid in demolition charges, which were covered in a variety of materials. Those in paper or Bakelite casings were tan or brown, those in metal field-grey (actually dark olive green) with white markings. The standard-sized cap wells were covered with a paper disc whose colour identified the filler – TNT, pink; picric acid, yellow; pentolite, green.

The bulk charges, developed in the 1920s, are described in the panel on this page. They included the *Bohrpatrone 28* and *Sprengkörper 28* packed in paper or Bakelite; the *Sprengbüchse 24*, which came in a pressure-resistant zinc case, allowing it to be used underwater; and 3kg and 10kg *Geballte Ladungen* (concentrated charges), in zinc cases with carrying handles. These self-contained charges were known collectively as *Einheitsladungen* (unitary charges).

The weight of special charges was included in their designations. The German use of hollow charges *(Hohlladungen)* early in the war came as a surprise, and was instrumental in some initial successes; the Germans made more use of hand-emplaced shaped charges than any other army.

Two very small 300g (1.75in × 3.5in) and 400g (2.8in × 3.1in) hollow-charge munitions were used to destroy gun barrels by wiring them on top with the two brackets provided.

The *Haft-Hohlladung 3kg* (magnetic hollow charge – *haft* means to cling) was a hand-delivered AT mine, also used against steel pillbox doors and shutters. Adopted in late 1942, it was a steel truncated cone attached to a triangular plywood base fitted with three pairs of magnets; a shaft holding the fuse and detonator doubled as a handle. Early models had a 4½-second delay, which was sometimes insufficient for the soldier to seek cover; a 7½-second fuse was introduced in May 1943.

German demolition charges (dimensions in inches)

Bohrpatrone 28 100g; TNT or picric acid; 1.2 diam × 3.9; paper-wrapped; 1 well
Bohrpatrone 28 100g; picric acid; 1.4 diam × 4.1; compressed paper case, Bakelite ends; 1 well
Sprengkörper 28 200g; TNT or picric acid; 1.5 × 2 × 2.75; paper-wrapped; 1 well
Sprengkörper 28 200g; picric acid; 1.8 × 2.2 × 3; Bakelite case; 1 well
Sprengbüchse 24 1kg; TNT or picric acid; 2.2 × 2.9 × 7.9; zinc case; 3 wells
Geballte Ladung 3kg; TNT; 3 × 6.5 × 7.7; zinc case; 3 or 5 wells
Geballte Ladung 10kg; TNT; 5 × 8.7 × 10; zinc case; 6 wells

For lack of a 'bangalore' or tube charge, a German pioneer shoves an expedient extended charge *(Gestreckteladung)* into barbed wire. This example is a plank with the heads of 14 stick grenades secured along it by wedging between wooden blocks; another type had 200g TNT charges wired on. (Private collection)

This charge could penetrate up to 140mm of armour and 50cm of concrete. The Germans' fear that the Soviets would develop a similar munition prompted them to begin aplying *Zimmerit* 'anti-magnetic' plaster to their armoured vehicles; the Soviets never did field a magnetic AT hand mine, but they did use captured examples in quantity. In early 1944 the *Haft-Hohlladung 3.5kg* was introduced, measuring 6in × 10.75in; similar in concept to the 3kg, it featured the warhead of a *Panzerfaust 60* AT rocket with the nose cone removed, fitted with magnets and a 7½-second delay igniter.

The 12.5kg hollow charge, a pre-war development, was a simple dome; without any means of stand-off it could only penetrate 4-plus inches of armour. The later, more bullet-shaped 13.5kg model had a side-mounted handle and three folding/telescoping 13.5in legs; this degree of stand-off allowed penetration of 9in of armour or up to 3.5ft of concrete. The massive 50kg (110.2lb) hollow-charge munition was so heavy that it was designed to be carried in two sections: the 19.1in-diameter, 5.4in-high base containing the cavity, and the 7.4in-high upper dome, with the fuse well and a concave bottom to fit over the base. Both sections had web carrying handles on the sides. Paratroopers were provided with a small two-wheel carrier to move it once on the ground. It could penetrate almost 10in of armour; if followed by a 12.5kg charge another 2in were penetrated, and if by another 50kg, a total 20in depth could be cut.

The German bangalore torpedo was the *Rohrladung, Stahl 3kg* (steel tube charge); '3kg' referred to the TNT filler, but the total weight was over 4kg (9 pounds). The 3.6ft-long sections were fastened together with integral bayonet-type locking lugs, and each charge was provided with a rounded nose cap. As a substitute for the *Rohrladung*, the *Gestreckteladung* (extended charge) might be used. This was a 100mm-wide plank, 2m or more long, with 200g block charges wired to it at 100mm–150mm intervals and often held in place by wood strips nailed along the sides of the board. Stick grenade heads, with the handles removed, were used in the same manner; the grenade at the user's end retained its handle containing the igniter. In either case the detonator

The Japanese favoured large bangalores, these examples being made of 3in-diameter bamboo poles packed with picric acid cartridges.

Reputed to have been taken on Corregidor Island, this photo shows Japanese assault engineers attacking a concrete pillbox with a Type 100 (1940) flamethrower.

wells of the charges/heads were oriented to the rear, and they all detonated sympathetically when the igniter charge exploded. A reasonable time delay was achieved with 200g charges by using the *Sprengkapselzünder* set; the use of a stick grenade as an initiator provided only a 4½-second delay. *Stangenladungen* (pole charges) were 2m–4m long; the charges were wired either to a braced square board centred across the end of the pole, or to a board attached like a paddle-blade.

The 3kg *Kugelladung* (ball charge) was intended for tossing into embrasures, but saw little use; it was a 6in steel sphere filled with 5.6lb of pentolite, with a 7½-second delay fuse and a web carrying handle on top.

Japan

The Japanese mainly used non-electric blasting caps, pull-cord friction fuse igniters, and several types of time-delay fuse and detcord, for which details are not available. The basic explosives used were TNT *(chakatusuyaku)* and picric acid *(shimose)* packed in tan waxed paper or light olive drab containers – see panel on this page for dimensions. They made much use of a crude cyclomite-based plastic explosive called *tanoyaku* issued in 100g cylinders wrapped in tissue paper and contained in a paper package.

The 10lb bangalore torpedo or demolition pipe *(hakai-to)*, filled with ten 110g TNT/cyclonite charges, came in a set of four (Plate E11). A screw-on cap at one end and a screw-in plug at the other were removed and the desired number of tubes screwed together. A separate detonator assembly with two blasting caps and a pull-cord friction igniter was delivered screwed into a blunt nose cone; this was removed and screwed into the last charge, and the cone to the first, and pulling the cord activated a 6- or 7-second delay fuse. Expedient bangalores, some quite large, were made by securing block charges along strips of bound bamboo.

A widely used demolition device was the Type 99 (1939) armour-destroying charge *(99 hako-bakurai)*. This hand-emplaced magnetic mine could penetrate up to 1⅛in of armour, relying on blast effect only. The disc-shaped charge (Plate E14) had four magnets spaced around the rim; issued in a canvas bag, it was known from its shape as the 'turtle'.

Japanese demolition charges (dimensions in inches)
Cylindrical charges:
    100g TNT or picric acid –
        1.2 diam × 4.6
    100g cheddite (76% ammonium perchlorate, 24% TNT) –
        1.2 diam × 4.6
    100g plastic explosive –
        1.5 diam × 4
Block charges:
    200g picric acid – 1 × 2.5 × 2.5
    400g TNT or picric acid –
        1.6 × 2 × 2.8
    400g cheddite – 1.6 × 2 × 2.8
    1kg TNT (zinc container) –
        2.2 × 3 × 8.2. Similar 3kg & 10kg charges reported.

Originally designed to attack pillbox doors, it was also used against the thin side and top armour of tanks. It weighed 2lb 10oz, contained 1lb 7oz of TNT, and was fitted with a 10-second delay percussion igniter (activated by striking on a solid surface). Mines were sometimes paired, being held together by their magnets, to penetrate up to 2.25in of armour. Sometimes two pairs of mines, with the magnets cut off, were fastened together (Plate E15) with 200g picric acid charges sandwiched between them, as a heavy demolition charge.

ASSAULT TACTICS APPLIED

Assault tactics at small-unit level were kept simple, owing to the limited experience of junior officers and the unavoidable difficulties of command and control in battle. The platoon tactics discussed here are based on the three-squad platoon.

Platoon **movement formations** were also simple. 'Line formation or skirmish line' had all squads aligned abreast and advancing, to provide maximum fire to the front. In 'column formation' squads moved in a file one behind the other, allowing rapid movement and easy control. The 'V or wedge' formation had one squad forward and two to the rear and flanks – suitable for when the enemy's location was unknown, since only one squad was exposed; if engaged, the trailing squads could come up on either or both sides of the point squad. In the 'inverted V or blunt wedge', two squads were forward and one centred behind; the third provided rear security, and could manoeuvre to the right or left to come on line or protect a flank. In both the wedge and inverted wedge one or more trailing squads could manoeuvre to outflank the enemy. A little-used formation was the 'echelon', with one squad in the lead and the second and third slanted progressively to the rear on one or the other side; this stepped formation provided fire to the front and flank, while allowing the second and third squads to move easily to the front or flank. Four-squad platoons might use 'box' or 'diamond' formations. Squads moving as part of these formations might assume different formations themselves: e.g., a platoon in line formation of squads might have the members of its squads themselves in line if engagement was imminent, or still in squad columns for rapidity and control.

The intervals between platoons, squads and individuals depended on the terrain, vegetation, visibility and tactical situation. In

From spring 1944 the US Marine Corps used a 13-man rifle squad comprising three 4-man fire teams. The teams worked in co-operation with one another, to fire and manoeuvre.

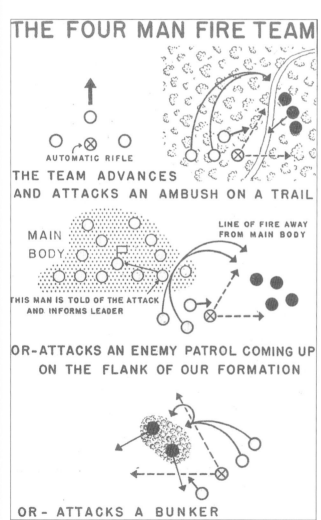

THE FOUR MAN FIRE TEAM

AUTOMATIC RIFLE

THE TEAM ADVANCES
AND ATTACKS AN AMBUSH ON A TRAIL

MAIN
BODY

LINE OF FIRE AWAY
FROM MAIN BODY

THIS MAN IS TOLD OF THE ATTACK
AND INFORMS LEADER

OR-ATTACKS AN ENEMY PATROL COMING UP
ON THE FLANK OF OUR FORMATION

OR - ATTACKS A BUNKER

desert and other open terrain, exposure dictated wide dispersal. In jungle and forest intervals were short, LMGs accompanied the forward riflemen, and clearings allowing the use of platoon/company mortars were scarce to non-existent. Ideally, each sub-unit could see the adjacent one, while individuals might be anything from a yard to 5 yards apart. Squad leaders placed themselves a few men back from the point when in column formations, and in the centre of line formations. The platoon commander typically followed the lead squad when in column; in other formations he placed himself centrally, moving about to where he could best observe and control. The platoon sergeant might do much the same, placing himself where the commander could not be, or bringing up the rear to prevent straggling.

Doctrine held that the frontal attack should be employed only when absolutely necessary. Ideally, attacks would be made from the flanks and rear, but this was not always possible owing to terrain and enemy dispositions – such attacks cannot be achieved against a continuous line of mutually supporting, in-depth defensive positions. The Western Allies and Germans used 'fire and movement' to advance: the squad MG group would move to a good position to engage the objective, while the rifle group manoeuvred to close with the enemy. Pairs of riflemen would alternate, one providing covering fire while the other moved, 'leap-frogging' forward by alternating bounds. A platoon did the same where it was feasible, with a squad providing covering fire for two squads advancing by bounds. When advancing up roads each sub-unit would split, with parallel files on either side prepared to take cover to the sides and return fire.

(Soviet and Japanese practice is discussed below – see 'Notes on National Practice'.)

Weapons employment and effects

The users of different weapons had to know how to integrate them into the sub-unit's firepower, and understand their effect on targets (especially 'hardened' targets). Not all weapons were appropriate in all situations, and users had to be flexible and imaginative rather than adhering rigidly to the manuals of doctrine.

Operation 'Epsom', Normandy, 26 June 1944: a very exposed platoon of 6th Bn Royal Scots Fusiliers advance through waist-high crops in light morning mist. One section can be seen in the left centre, and part of another in the right foreground, so the platoon is using a classic 'V or wedge' formation with one squad up and two back. In the left middle distance the lone rifleman between the sections should be the platoon commander or platoon sergeant, in the traditional central position from where he can see and control movement. (IWM B 5951)

The common infantry **rifle** was a bolt-action weapon of either 7.62–8mm (.30–.32cal) or 6.5mm (.25cal). The British Commonwealth used a 10-round magazine rifle, most other armies a five-round magazine, and the US an eight-round semi-automatic rather than a bolt action (the Germans and Soviets did have some semi-automatics, but made only limited use of them). Defenders are normally under cover and do not often present themselves as targets, so the penetration capability of rifle-calibre weapons, including machine guns, was critical. If they could not shoot through logs, masonry, two layers of sandbags, interior building walls and ceilings or dense brush, then their value was limited; the 6.5mm rifles used by Japan and Italy were particularly wanting in this respect.

A practised man with a five-shot bolt-action rifle could crack out 8–10 aimed· shots per minute including reloading; for virtually unaimed suppressive fire a higher rate could be achieved for short periods. A platoon with 20–30 rifles could thus lay down significant suppressive fire; how much actual damage it did is debatable, but it did have a psychological impact and forced defenders to keep their heads down. In theory, men were supposed to fire their weapons during the actual assault rush; in practice this was seldom done, since in close combat it is awkward to fire – much less reload – on the run, and soldiers preferred to run to the next available cover before firing. Once within the enemy positions rifles were effective, if somewhat restricted when in confined quarters. Bayonet wounds were quite rare, even though Russian and Japanese doctrine called for bayonets to be fixed at all times.

Among the infantry of most armies **sub-machine guns** (machine pistols, machine carbines) were scarce, and often only carried – if at all – by platoon and squad leaders. Only the Red Army made extensive use of SMGs, issuing them on a wider scale – to up to half the members of the infantry platoon – from 1943. Standard US Army and Marine rifle platoons, and the Japanese, had no SMGs; most German squad leaders had them, as did their British Commonwealth counterparts by 1942/43. Some units naturally obtained 'unofficial' SMGs, valuing them as close-combat weapons for their rate of fire, compactness, and ease of use at close quarters. However, the pistol-calibre bullets had poor penetration and effective range was 50 yards at most.

Squad automatic weapons of the era were bipod-mounted **light machine guns** of similar capabilities, although their magazine capacity affected their sustained fire: US, 20 rounds; British Commonwealth and Japanese, 30; Soviet, 47; and German, belts of 50 rounds which could be linked to give longer sustained fire capability. Some LMGs were provided with a spare quick-change barrel. The value of LMGs was their suppressive-fire capability, for instance against embrasures and small enemy groups. Regardless of exaggerated claims, the realistic effective combat range of rifles and LMGs was not much beyond 300 yards, and most exchanges of fire between infantry took place at less than 100 yards.

Company and battalion **machine guns** were tripod-mounted, with either water-cooled (British, some US) or air-cooled heavy barrels allowing sustained longer-range fire. They were most effective if employed in pairs for covering and suppressive fire; indirect fire was little used.

Rifle-calibre bullet penetration (in inches, at 200 yards' range) This table is based on the US .30cal, 174-grain, M1 ball cartridge; this was slightly more powerful than the British .303in, Soviet 7.62mm, German 7.9mm and Japanese 7.7mm.

Armour plate	0.3*
Concrete (plain)	2
Brick masonry	5**
Gravel	8
Dry sand	12
Moist sand	14
Solid oak	20
Earth	30
Greasy clay	60***

* = .30cal armour-piercing bullet penetrated 0.6in

** = Greater penetration through the softer mortar

*** = Maximum – great variation depending on consistency

(continued on page 41)

US FLAMETHROWER ASSAULT TEAM, TARAWA, 1943

B

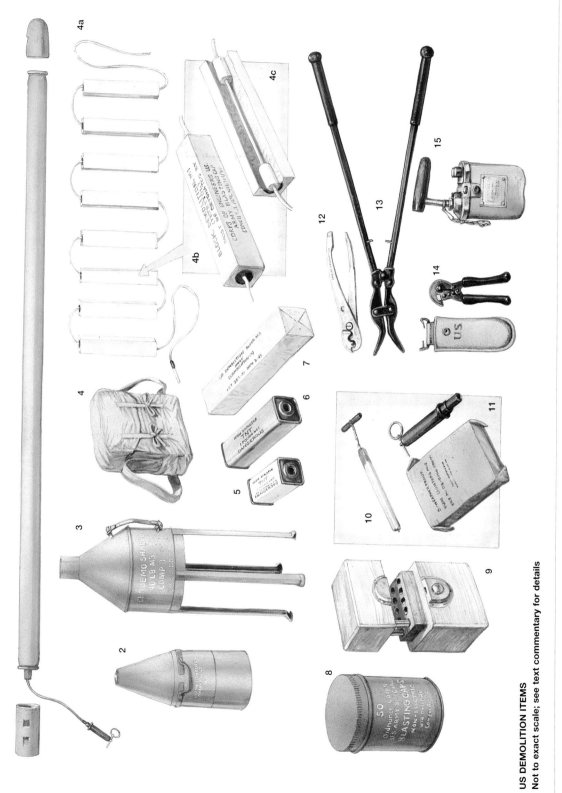

US DEMOLITION ITEMS

Not to exact scale; see text commentary for details

C

BRITISH & SOVIET DEMOLITION ITEMS
Not to exact scale; see text commentary for details

1

2   P.E.N⁰.2

3   N.G. 73.A.T. Mk.1. M.B.Co.40

4

5

6   T.N.T/AC 1/A

7

8

9

10

11   ТОЛ ПРЕССОВАННЫЙ   вес. 75 кг

12   МЕЛИНИТ   вес. 200 грамм

13   ТОЛ В.ПРЕССОВАННЫМ   в.е.с. 300 грам

14   ТОЛ 5кг

15

16

D

GERMAN & JAPANESE DEMOLITION ITEMS
Not to exact scale; see text commentary for details

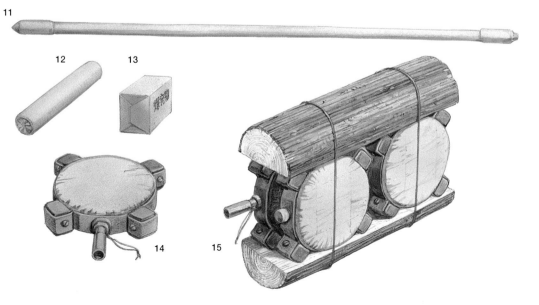

E

BRITISH MOUSE-HOLING CHARGE, 1944–45

F

Hand grenades were expended in great numbers in the assault, against fighting positions, pillboxes, bunkers, caves and within buildings. Most riflemen carried two to four grenades, but resupply had to be continuous, and this was not always achieved. 'Offensive' grenades relied on blast and generated few fragments, so as to limit the danger to the attackers; 'defensive' grenades generated numerous fragments, and were supposed to be used against exposed attackers while the throwers were under cover. The so-called defensive fragmentation grenades were much the more effective for clearing enemy positions, and in practice men used whatever was available regardless of circumstances. Slip-on fragmentation sleeves were available to convert some types of offensive grenades. White phosphorus (WP) grenades were ruptured by a bursting charge, igniting the WP and immediately creating a dense cloud of white smoke. They were also terribly effective when attacking enemy positions, since they showered droplets of WP burning at 5,000°F (2,760°C); these burned through flesh and were difficult to extinguish – attempting to wipe it off only smeared the blazing goo further. Grenade fuse delays varied: US, 4–5 seconds; British, 4 seconds; Soviet, 3¼–4¼ seconds; German, 4½ seconds; and Japan, 4–5 seconds. To prevent a grenade from being thrown back, a grenadier might hold it for 2–3 seconds after arming it before throwing; since neither perception of time nor fuse delays were ever entirely reliable, this was occasionally a fatal mistake.

Both anti-tank and anti-personnel **rifle grenades** were useful for attacking field fortifications, among other targets. Whether used for

Assault troops received rations and water in their assembly area, passing ammunition points where they could load up with ammo and grenades.

41

Time and situation permitting, the platoon commander and squad leaders reconnoitred the route to the 'line of departure', and tried to study their objective through binoculars for any visible details. Assault infantry should be briefed about their objective and its known defences in as great a degree of detail as possible. The means might be sketch maps, or simple lines scratched in the dirt – as here, by the leader of a squad from 120th Infantry, US 30th Div in Normandy in mid-August 1944. If the information and the time were available, a more elaborate terrain model might be made using scraped-up earth, sticks and stones; there might even be a chance to rehearse their moves; but all too often, attacks had to be made at short notice and with little useful information. (NARA)

direct or indirect fire their accuracy was marginal, and their effective range was usually less than 100 yards. Platoon and company **anti-tank weapons** were useful against fortifications, up to a point; designed to penetrate armour, they were less effective against concrete, earth and logs. This was especially true of AT rifles, but later shoulder-fired rocket launchers or projectors with shaped-charge warheads, such as the bazooka, PIAT and *Panzerfaust*, were more effective.

Mortars were relatively light for their punch, easily achieved rapid rates of fire, and were portable enough for the crews to follow close behind assault troops. They were area rather than point weapons, expending prodigious amounts of ammunition, and the rounds were heavy for man-transport. At company and battalion level they provided rapidly responsive fires without the need to request artillery support. The rounds from 50mm–60mm (c.2in) light mortars had insufficient weight to penetrate the overhead cover of field fortifications; that required at least medium mortars in the 81mm (c.3in) range, and the contemporary scarcity of fraction-of-a-second delay fuses lessened even their penetration. Company mortars were seldom parcelled out to platoons, but kept for concentrated and controlled fire.

The Russians, Germans and Japanese employed **infantry guns**, light howitzers that could be manhandled by troops over most terrain. They could deliver indirect fire, but their real value was in accurate direct fire against MG nests and other positions.

Tanks and SP assault guns were excellent for grinding through barbed wire and knocking out MG nests; they offered protection from small arms, fragments, small-calibre guns and anti-personnel mines, and could push though moderate obstacles. However, they were vulnerable to AT guns and rockets, mines, and close artillery hits; unsuitable terrain and heavy man-made obstacles could seriously restrict their movement, and in built-up areas the limited elevation of their guns often prevented them from engaging targets on upper floors.[2] When tanks did succeed in negotiating the terrain and obstacles they could use their main armament and MGs to engage enemy positions, providing valuable support (and psychological encouragement) to assaulting infantry. Other AFVs used to support the assault included halftracks mounting guns, and various specialized engineer assault vehicles such as dozer and flail (mine-clearing) tanks, armoured engineer assault vehicles with large-calibre, short-range guns, and flamethrower tanks. When it was necessary to crack extremely robust fortifications or caves, even towed and SP heavy artillery might be manoeuvred into position for short-range direct fire.

The **flamethrower** proved to be one of the most effective weapons for reducing fortifications; all of the major combatants employed them to varying degrees. Flamethrowers were not easy to use: they were heavy (typically at least 70lb), awkward to carry, and required special pumps and equipment to pressure the propellant tank. The ignition systems were notoriously unreliable; they were very short-ranged (15–20 yards); and as unthickened petrol or oil was used they only provided a few short bursts before the fuel was expended. Flamethrower tanks saw some use by the US, British and Germans, with a flamegun replacing the turret gun or the bow MG; these had a longer range – 60, 70, sometimes over 100 yards – and longer fuel duration. Their main advantage was that they could move in close to the target without exposing troops.

Assault preparations

When attacking fortified positions protected by obstacles a great deal of planning, preparation and co-ordination were necessary, its extent varying according to the echelon, and the information and time available.

The platoon was assigned its mission and objective by the company commander, and moved to an assembly area to prepare. Artillery and mortar fires were registered by forward observers, supporting weapons positioned, and exact fire missions established, much of this work being done at the battalion or regimental echelon. At platoon level, co-ordination was discussed with any attachments such as engineers and company machine guns. The starting position and time, and the

Artillery and mortar forward observers were crucial to the assault, precisely directing fires on to any specific targets that were stalling the attack – simply dropping a barrage on the whole area did little good. The control of fire involved designating targets for individual artillery units, the time and duration of their fire mission, and subsequent missions. Once the attack started radio and telephone communications could not be relied on, so the timing of lifting or shifting fires was crucial. Artillery forward observers accompanied US and British Commonwealth infantry; Soviet, German and Japanese practice was for observers to remain in observation posts behind them.

[2] For extensive discussion of these points, see Elite 124, *World War II Infantry Anti-Tank Tactics*

times when support fires would commence, lift or shift were confirmed, together with the location of the company command group, aid station and ammunition and supply points. The most critical aspect was co-ordination of the plan with supporting MGs, mortars, infantry guns and tanks, as well as with adjacent units.

The great importance of tank–infantry co-ordination was learned the hard way. Early in the war tanks and infantry were envisioned as separate arms, but it was soon found that they relied on one another and needed to work in close co-operation. Tankers had to know where the infantry were, where to link up with them and what their mission was, so they could engage the necessary targets at the appropriate times. Communications had to be worked out – tank and infantry radios often could not be set on common frequencies; so infantry radios were provided to tankers, and field telephones were mounted on the rear of tanks for following infantrymen to use. Verbal communication against the din of running engines and battle noise was impossible; infantrymen might mark targets with tracer rounds, coloured smoke and flares, but due to the dust and smoke, and the tank crews' very limited visibility, this was often inadequate. Direct co-ordination at the lowest levels was necessary to success; if a tank platoon/troop was attached to a rifle company, the armour commander had to co-ordinate directly with the rifle company and platoon commanders – even individual tank commanders with squad leaders.

The troops needed to know more than just what and where the objective was. Identified obstacles and defensive positions were described, as well as the orientation and suspected fields of fire of the defenders' weapons. All this information had been gleaned from reconnaissance patrols, either by the assault unit or another, or from

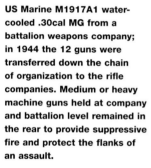

US Marine M1917A1 water-cooled .30cal MG from a battalion weapons company; in 1944 the 12 guns were transferred down the chain of organization to the rifle companies. Medium or heavy machine guns held at company and battalion level remained in the rear to provide suppressive fire and protect the flanks of an assault.

Tank support was valuable, but not always available. Some Sherman tanks mounting 105mm howitzers, in place of high-velocity 75mm or 76mm guns, were provided to the HQ companies of tank battalions. For the assault role about 250 Sherman 'Jumbos' were specially converted, with a massively armoured turret and extra hull protection; this 76mm M4A3E2 was photographed with 37th Tank Bn, 4th US Armd Div in Alzey, Germany, on 20 March 1945. (NARA)

aerial photos and map reconnaissance; enemy locations might also be determined by probes and feint attacks, so the defenders would reveal their positions by returning fire. Often, however, little information was available; if the enemy's deception and camouflage efforts were successful – especially in heavy vegetation – then only an approximate guess might be possible as to the trace of his front line.

Platoon and squad movement formations were specified, along with the positioning of squad LMGs and any attached crew-served weapons. Demolition charges, wire-cutters, mine probes and any other tools and equipment were assigned to specific individuals, with alternates chosen to take over if these became casualties. The platoons and squads were task-organized internally; the integrity of squads might be maintained, but they might also be broken up to form breaching, assault and cover or support groups.

One or more breaching groups, perhaps comprised of or augmented by engineers, would be formed for each lane to be cleared; a steady leader, trusted by the troops, was placed in charge. For deliberate minefield breaching this group might be as large as a whole engineer platoon. The breaching group survivors would back up the assault groups once they passed through the gap, and might take over from or reinforce the assault group.

The assault group was usually the largest element, and heavily armed. Any platoon had its real fighters, experienced veterans who did not hesitate to use their weapons; the platoon commander would personally lead this group. Sometimes two assault groups might be organized and assigned different parts of the objective. If a platoon had relatively inexperienced squad leaders the platoon commander and platoon sergeant might each take command of a group – either two assault groups, or an assault and a support group. Actions on the objective were discussed, and if time permitted rehearsals were conducted by assault and breaching groups. Alternates were assigned for all key jobs, and if possible every man needed to know what the others' assignments were.

Supporting fires

Each echelon possessed a fire support element; during a given unit's mission it might receive support from a number of echelons, and these all had to be co-ordinated. Typically, regardless of echelon, two of a unit's sub-units led the attack with one in reserve or support. At company level the two assault platoons generally received support from the same source, because of their narrow attack frontage. At battalion level and higher, one of the assault companies would attack the main objective and the other a secondary objective. The term 'secondary' did not indicate a lower-value objective: its capture was just as important, since its occupation protected the flank of the main attack and provided it with fire support, as well as assisting a further advance once the main objective was secured.

The main assault company would receive the lion's share of fire support from battalion and possibly regimental assets. For example, it might have the battalion mortar platoon and two of the three MG platoons firing in direct support. The platoon or section of AT or infantry guns attached to the battalion from regiment might be placed in direct support of the main attack company, as might much of the battalion's allocation of heavy mortar and artillery support. If a tank platoon was allocated to the battalion it might support either the main attack or – if restricted by terrain or obstacles on that frontage – the secondary attack; in the latter case the tanks could support the main attack by fires from a flank. The main attack unit might be assigned a narrower frontage to give a denser concentration of firepower.

During the course of any assault its emphasis could be shifted from the main to the secondary objective if the main effort failed or bogged down – the general rule was not to reinforce defeat. Instead, the secondary attack could be reinforced by the reserve, and supporting fires shifted, so the positioning of crew-served weapons was critical. Machine guns either accompanied the assault troops or were positioned to fire from the rear, through gaps between units or overhead if the terrain provided sufficient elevation. Company mortars were emplaced close behind the forward units to maximize their range and ease their rapid movement forward; battalion mortars were further back, to allow them to cover the battalion front, although they might be further forward to support the main assault company. Infantry guns might support by indirect fire, like the mortars, but they were also valuable as direct-fire weapons to engage fighting positions, and thus were usually placed well forward – the same applied to AT guns employed in this way. Regardless of the weapon, lines of fire were critical, so as not to endanger friendly troops and to place effective fire on the necessary targets, bearing in mind that advancing infantry might mask these.

To survive an assault in a fortified or built-up area infantrymen needed to operate in pairs or threes, watching each others' backs as they fired and manoeuvred.

Down at platoon level, organic and attached weapons were often organized into a support group, usually under the platoon sergeant. There might be more than one such group: for example, a light mortar might be positioned to the rear, though probably on line of sight with the target area, with an AT rifle or bazooka closer in for covering fire. Sometimes two or more of the squad LMGs were set up under a single leader to cover the breaching and assault groups, and one or more attached company MGs might be positioned elsewhere to take advantage of their range. Machine guns were often established in different positions across the platoon's sector, to achieve different lines of fire on different targets.

Artillery preparation was comparatively brief compared to the norms of World War I. Rather than barraging a whole area for prolonged periods, more precise targeting was preferred (if target-location allowed); however, in many instances saturation and 'marching' barrages were still necessary. At division level, light artillery engaged frontline targets while medium artillery blasted positions in the rear. Corps artillery might reinforce either mission, as well as providing counterbattery fire.[3]

Smoke-screens were valuable for blinding the enemy or screening friendly positions, advances and withdrawals. (Conversely, the attackers might be blinded and disoriented by their own smoke as they advanced – it is extremely difficult to maintain direction and avoid obstacles when dense smoke reduces visibility to a couple of yards.) Even a thin screen was valuable, as optical weapons sights aimed into it magnified the white haze, thus neutralizing them. When saturated with smoke defending AFVs often withdrew, because of the fear of close-in infantry attack under its cover. Smoke could be delivered by hand and rifle grenades, burning pots and candles, ground- or vehicle-mounted generators,

---

[3] Divisional artillery: US, 105mm & 155mm howitzers; British Commonwealth, 25pdr (87mm) gun-howitzer & 5.5in (140mm) gun; Soviet, 76mm gun, 122mm & 152mm howitzers; Germany, 10.5cm & 15cm howitzers, 10cm gun; Japan, 7.5cm gun, 10cm howitzer.

mortars, artillery, aerial bombs and aircraft spraying. Its effectiveness was greatly dependent on wind speed and direction, air temperature and humidity, the means of delivery and the type of smoke compound. Some compounds, especially WP, burned hotter than others and rose and dispersed faster. Smoke had to be refreshed depending on the screen's desired duration, and individual smoke rounds were fired to 'touch up' holes.

THE ASSAULT

How the assault was conducted depended on the distance to be covered. An approach march or movement to contact might have to be executed; the units might have to pass through enemy patrols, covering forces, outposts, and the full range of obstacles, while subject to long-range attack by air and artillery. At the other extreme, when the front lines were in close proximity the assault unit would launch its attack immediately or as soon as engaged.

Assault units would move to their assault positions or final assembly areas, which offered cover and concealment out of small-arms range. By this point all preparations had been accomplished; preparatory fires commenced at a specified time, and the attack was launched from the 'line of departure' or 'start line' at 'H-hour' or 'zero hour'. Some manoeuvres might commence before this, such as the despatch of breaching parties or feint and divisionary attacks.

The success of an assault depended as much upon the morale of the troops – their motivation, their state of rest and rations, the quality of their leadership, and the weather – as on the employment of supporting weapons and the scheme of manoeuvre. Assault units would cross their lines of departure either at a specified time or on receiving an order. Except in dense vegetation they could expect to come under fire within 300–500 yards of the enemy positions, possibly further out by artillery and mortars. For this reason they moved slowly and kept concealed as long as possible; assault troops and accompanying crew-served weapons did not fire unless they encountered enemy outposts or patrols. They relied on supporting fires to suppress the enemy and 'walk' them on to the objective, and only opened fire if necessary to continue gaining ground when supporting fires failed to suppress the defenders.

Most armies taught that it was unnecessary for individuals and sub-units to maintain alignment; attempting to do so slowed the advance and presented better targets so, once engaged, units were to advance irrespective of the location or actions of adjacent units. Great emphasis was placed on maintaining the advance: assault troops had to keep moving forward, neither halting to care for wounded, nor getting distracted by firefights with by-passed defenders, nor paying attention to exposed flanks. They advanced at a walk, a run, in short bounds from cover to cover, or low-crawled, depending on the situation. A rush of anything more than 50 yards invited excessive casualties.

Once within the enemy positions close-range shoot-outs, hand grenades, hand-delivered demolitions, bayonets and hand-to-hand combat dictated the result. If this was successful, positions were cleared and searched, enemy weapons gathered up, and constant vigilance was maintained, since the attackers might be engaged from any direction. Even when the objective was cleared it was not yet secure, and the assault unit had to consolidate. They might reorganize into their normal structure, dissolving breaching, assault and support groups, or might reorganize to continue the assault. All troops were accounted for, wounded treated and evacuated, prisoners collected and sent to the rear, ammunition redistributed, and men and crew-served weapons positioned to face a counter-attack. Often the enemy would counter-attack as soon as possible to hamper the occupiers' consolidation, even if the effort could not be strong enough to actually eject them. This might be followed by a more substantial counter-attack by a reserve unit. If the defenders were obviously weak, the attackers might pursue them by fire (i.e. shoot them as they ran), physically pursue, or continue the attack toward the next objective – even if this was not planned, an aggressive commander would exploit the opportunity.

NOTES ON NATIONAL PRACTICE

United States

The basic concept specified that when the platoon came under fire further advance was by fire-and-manoeuvre. The enemy was pinned by frontal and/or flanking fire from one of the squads, and the other squads leap-frogged forwards from cover to cover. Weak spots were sought out, which the manoeuvring elements would hit. Depending on the situation and terrain, one or both of the manoeuvring squads might then provide covering fire while the supporting squad manoeuvred.

The Marines in the **Pacific** were among the first US forces to have to deal with extensive, in-depth, mutually supporting defences in close, broken terrain. The reduction of pillboxes and caves demanded a series of small individual battles, so the assault elements had to be self-supporting. In the early operations in the Solomons the terrain made tank support difficult or impossible, and when they were present the light tanks too often outran the infantry and fell victim to close-in infantry attacks. It was quickly learned that a squad had to accompany and protect each tank.

Demolitions were essential for defeating pillboxes and caves. From the beginning the Marines included a dedicated demolitions corporal in each rifle platoon (something no other army considered); he was responsible for training all platoon members in the use of demolitions. Some Marines taped demolition charges with short delay fuses to 60mm and 81mm mortar rounds and chucked them into caves.) For the late 1943 Tarawa assault the 2nd Marine Division's engineer battalion formed 6-man assault teams armed with flamethrowers and demolitions for attachment to rifle platoons (see Plate B). This was the first time bazookas and flamethrowers were available, along with M4 Sherman medium tanks, and on Tarawa the absolute necessity for close tank–infantry co-ordination was driven home.

Typically two or three Japanese pillboxes, each with one to three MGs, were positioned for mutual covering fire; they in turn were covered by snipers, and by infantry, MGs and 'knee mortars' in foxholes scattered throughout the area. To attack one pillbox was to receive fire from multiple directions, so these covering positions would have to be dealt with first. Then, while some elements of the platoon suppressed

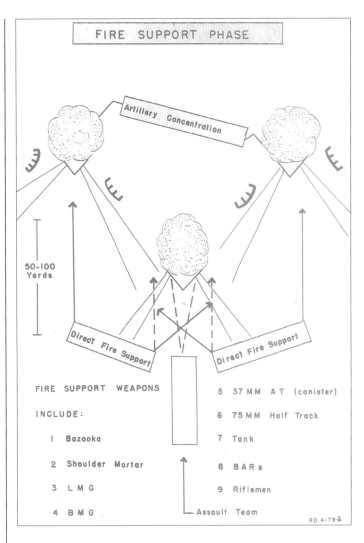

FIRE SUPPORT PHASE

50-100 Yards

Artillery Concentration

Direct Fire Support

Direct Fire Support

FIRE SUPPORT WEAPONS

INCLUDE:

1   Bazooka

2   Shoulder Mortar

3   LMG

4   BMG

5   37 MM AT (canister)

6   75 MM Half Track

7   Tank

8   BARs

9   Riflemen

Assault Team

RD 4179-2

Diagram showing the US Marine concept for assaulting mutually supportive pillboxes with heavy firepower. While artillery is concentrated on the covering pillboxes, two rifle squads provide suppressive fire ('direct fire support') on all three, while a third assaults the first pillbox directly. The potentially available arsenal of fire support weapons is listed.

remaining positions, an assault group supported by MGs, AT guns and mortars would attack the main position with grenades and demolitions. The Marines made good use of the 37mm AT gun against pillboxes; its high explosive (HE) and armour-piercing (AP) rounds were largely ineffective but its canister rounds stripped away camouflage to reveal the pillbox for attack with other weapons.

For the Marshalls assault in early 1944 the Marines organized two 20-man assault sections for each regiment; these were composed of 5-man BAR, bazooka, and demolitions groups, with an MG gun team in one group and a flamethrower team in another, and these groups were brought forward to take out particularly difficult positions. In April 1944 Marine battalions had enough flamethrowers and demolition kits to allot one to each squad, but it was recognized that they were better operated by specialists. On Peleliu the 1st Marine Division organized 60-man battalion weapons platoons, each with three flamethrower groups (two flamethrowers), three bazooka groups and three heavy demolitions groups. This was also done on Iwo Jima, and was finally formalized in May 1945, with a 55-man assault platoon organized in each battalion. This platoon had a 10-man headquarters, and three sections for attachment one to each rifle company; a section had two 7-man squads with 2-man flamethrower, bazooka and demolition teams. The Army in the Pacific formed similar teams: for example, the 7th Infantry Division on Kwajalein picked 16 men in each company for flamethrower and demolition training, then separated them into small teams for attachment to platoons.

The Marine technique was to employ up to a company to suppress adjacent enemy positions, along with supporting fires from every available weapon and echelon. The assault platoon, reinforced by a specialist assault team, would manoeuvre to attack the selected position. Terrain permitting, tanks might advance ahead of the infantry to blast positions, with the infantry to the rear covering them from close-in attack. Besides tanks they employed halftrack-mounted 75mm guns (later replaced by SP 105mm M7 howitzers, on Okinawa). If few enemy AT guns were present or surviving, tanks moved up to fire into positions point-blank; flamethrower tanks proved especially valuable.

With adjacent positions suppressed, the assault teams would move in with rifles, BARs, MGs and rifle-grenades to saturate embrasures perhaps screened by burning-type white smoke grenades. Flamethrowers and bazookas would move in as close as possible, accompanied by a BAR, to 'blowtorch' and blast the gun ports, before a demo-man rushed in to finish the pillbox off with a satchel change – the 'corkscrew'. To reduce exposure of flame-gunners they sometimes fired from behind cover, directed by an observer on the flank and out of the target's field of fire. Units learned not to let insignificant groups of diehards tie them down, and only took out positions that were halting the advance; guards were left behind to warn follow-up reserve units, who mopped up the hold-outs.

One of the first challenges faced by the Army in **France** was the Normandy *bocage* country – a compartmented maze of fields, orchards and pastures separated by thick, tall hedgerows growing out of earth and rock berms up to 5ft high, topped with trees. Ditch-lined roads and wagon tracks ran throughout the area, enclosed on both sides by such banked hedgerows. The enclosed fields could be anything from small patches to several hundred yards on a side – square, rectangular, triangular, and laid out in irregular patterns. The Germans dug well-camouflaged weapons positions and riflemen's holes into the hedgerows. Observation between fields was impossible, and an attacking force had no idea what was behind the next or adjacent hedgerows; the only way to approach one was by crossing open fields. The Germans dug their hedgerow positions to no discernible trace, but in rough chequerboard patterns for mutual support.

As American tactics evolved, fields were attacked individually with tank support, while mortars and artillery suppressed the hedgerows of intervening fields. Improvised hedgerow-cutting ploughs were attached to tanks so they could simply burst through – a quicker means than the engineer-emplaced demolitions otherwise used to blow gaps. Whether the gap was cut or blown, a tank would approach the hedgerow and

Only the US and British Commonwealth armies employed tank-dozers like this M4 Sherman with an M1 dozer blade; they were extremely useful for breaching (or simply burying) several kinds of obstacle. (NARA, courtesy Steven Zaloga)

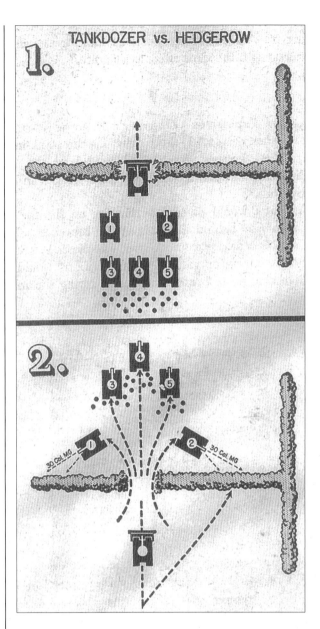

TANKDOZER vs. HEGDEROW

One of various tactics developed to deal with the Normandy hedgerows. (1) A tank-dozer, or a Sherman fitted with a locally made cutter, bursts a gap through a banked hedgerow for the following tank platoon and rifle platoon. (2) It then withdraws, moving to cut another gap if necessary. The first two tanks through the gap turn right and left to cover the gapped hedgerow and flanking hedges with MG fire, while the others and the rifle platoon move ahead to suppress and clear the next hedge line.

sweep the opposite hedgerow with traversing MG fire. A squad or platoon would advance into the next field, peppering the far hedgerow, while a mortar observer with the tanks directed fire from a 60mm. Engineers emplaced the charges, and the tank pulled back while they were blown. The tank then advanced through the gap to the next hedgerow, covered by the infantry, and the process was repeated.

The greatest challenge came in October 1944 when US troops reached the Siegfried Line (*Westwall*) protecting the German border. This formidable belt of mutually supporting bunkers and AT obstacles, reinforced by field works, caused real apprehension. The true value of a permanent fortified line was that it could be reinforced by field fortifications and backed by mobile counter-attack forces. The Germans accomplished the former; however, by this time they lacked the latter.

The defensive bunkers were massively strong but often had limited fields of fire, and – designed for pre-war ordnance – they could not house the larger AT weapons. US platoons formed assault teams and conducted training with supporting tanks, two or three tanks usually supporting a rifle platoon.

Artillery and mortars blanketed the target and adjacent bunkers as the assault troops moved into position; these fires would not damage the bunkers, but suppressed the infantry dug in around them and blasted away concealing vegetation. Bazookas and ground and tank MGs kept the embrasures under fire until the flamethrowers and demolition men had moved up. It was often found that it was only necessary for the flamethrower to shoot off a jet of flame in view of the embrasure, and the defenders filed out with their hands up. The more dedicated suffered concentrated bursts of flaming thickened fuel gushing through embrasures, while demolition men thrust pole charges through the embrasures and against doors – by that point it was too late to ask for quarter. Self-propelled 155mm guns might be moved within a few hundred yards of bunkers, firing directly into them from outside effective small-arms range. Another technique was for a tank-dozer to pile earth against the embrasures and doors and simply bury the pillbox; once word of this spread, the defenders often either fled or surrendered when dozer-tanks approached. Most bunkers were destroyed by follow-on engineers placing multiple 550lb charges inside to prevent their reoccupation.

US forces maximized their advantage in artillery (and where feasible, naval gunfire), to blast the defenders out or stun and disorient them prior to throwing infantry into the assault. Tanks, tank-destroyers and SP artillery were liberally employed for direct fire. Commanders were encouraged to use their imagination in tactical applications of weapons other than their originally planned means.

British Commonwealth

At the beginning of the war the British doctrine was for advancing troops to keep moving and not fire their weapons unless enemy fire was so heavy as to force them to take cover; the artillery was to 'walk' them on to the objective. In this new war such hopes proved optimistic, and a system of 'battle drills' was soon adopted, providing prescribed procedures for different types of actions at each echelon. From 1941 onwards the British and other Commonwealth forces perfected battle drills, and paid a great deal of attention to small-unit tactics and techniques. Each man was assigned a specific duty to focus on during the inevitable confusion of battle.

On the European fronts, a rifle platoon would be joined at its forming-up place by assault sappers armed with bangalores and pole charges (and, if available, one to three tanks). Battle drill envisioned a squad divided into a rifle group and a Bren LMG group. They would manoeuvre around to the flanks of the enemy position, alternating their movements, until the rifle group was in a favourable position to assault and the Bren gun in a good covering position. In practice, an assault group was more often formed from the most reliable and experienced riflemen under the platoon commander, and backed by the sappers, while the three Brens and the 2in mortar – for smoke bombs – were grouped under the platoon sergeant. A few less experienced (or less reliable) men were assigned under a section leader to bring up ammunition, check any wounded and protect the rear. One reason for such an organization was that a platoon in prolonged combat might often field only about 20 men. Another method was to divide the platoon as follows for an assault on a fixed position:

Mortars provided important support; they could suppress fire from adjacent enemy positions covering the approaches to the objective, lay smoke, or engage enemy counter-attacks. This 4.2in Mk 1 mortar from the support battalion of British 3rd Div in Normandy, transported by a tracked carrier, is essentially identical in design to the lighter Brandt-type mortars of 3in/80mm calibre used by infantry battalions of all the combatant armies. Note the incremental propellant charges wired between the vanes of the 20lb bomb at right; this 'pocket artillery' for the infantry could reach ranges out to 2¼ miles. (IWM B5575)

During urban fighting, Red Army soldiers rush across a gap to the next building. Assault troops usually travelled light, dumping their packs and other unnecessary gear, so the case carried by the man in the centre may contain demolitions equipment. (Courtesy Nik Cornish)

No.1 Section and Platoon HQ – fire section
No. 2 Section, with PIAT, plus four sappers – cut-off section
No. 3 Section – pillbox clearing section.

The fire section opened heavy fire, with the mortar laying smoke. The cut-off section and sappers moved forward, keeping wide of the fire section, with the PIAT engaging the pillbox from further to a flank. The sappers emplaced the bangalores in the wire, throwing smoke grenades to thicken up the screen. The cut-off section rushed the gap and took up positions around the pillbox, killing any enemy dug-in around it and preventing reinforcement. The sappers placed pole charges in the embrasures, and joined the cut-off section. On the bursting of the pole charges the clearing section entered the pillbox with grenades and small arms; the pillbox door might be blown with demolitions. The platoon consolidated, and the sappers widened and marked the gap in the wire.

As the Germans went on the defensive they became adept at constructing AT ditches; these normally had vertical faces on both sides, requiring both to be collapsed with demolitions before a tank could cross. The simplest method was for sappers to break down the faces with picks and shovels, the shovel heads being modified by bending the blades at right angles so sappers could pull the earth down towards them. For deep ditches or hard soil, 25lb demolition charges were set in a line along both sides, 12ft long with intervals of 9in or less, at a distance from the lip equal to one-half the depth; double charges would be placed at the ends of the lines, and the charges either buried or tamped with sandbags. If the faces were revetted, charges were propped with struts against the face one-third its depth from the bottom. All charges were connected by cordex and detonated simultaneously, thus blowing the walls into the ditch, partially filling it and creating rough ramps, to be shaped with picks and shovels. As the tank gunned its engine to climb out the rear of the tracks might dig into the loose bottom soil; so 12ft-long brushwood fascines were prepared, 14in in diameter at the ends and tightly bound to 8in in the centre, with spares stockpiled for repairs as more tanks rolled through.

The Australians in the South-West Pacific had learned a great deal from the Japanese on New Guinea in 1942, and also integrated lessons learned in North Africa in 1940–41. In the jungle, even company assaults demanded that two or three platoons conduct their own individual attacks within the larger plan. There was usually little supporting fire due to the limitations of dense vegetation; sometimes a pair of medium MGs might support a company or platoon attack. The Australians taped small demolition charges to grenades for greater effect against pillboxes; this idea was refined, and a 'blast attachment' was adopted – a tin filled with 1lb of TNT or ammonal that screwed to the base of a Mills bomb.

Soviet Union

Early in Russia's war there was little experience or skill among commanders at any echelon. Attacks on German positions were launched by mobs of ill-trained riflemen herded across open ground (sometimes drunk); they would either roll right over German positions, or, more often, be chopped down in droves. By 1943–45 the Red Army had come a long way since the sacrificial charges of 1941; new leadership, field experience and equipment greatly improved planning skills and operational competence.

Nevertheless, throughout the war the Red Army often practised steamroller tactics, costly in manpower and placing heavy reliance on supporting weapons, especially artillery and tanks. The rifle platoon in other armies frequently served as the primary sub-unit around which assault groups were organized, but in the Red Army it was the company that formed such detachments. The rifle platoon seldom operated independently, being viewed as simply a component of the company, just as the squad was considered a component of the platoon in Western armies.

In the normal attack, platoons simply formed up in skirmish lines with a 100-yard front for a four-squad platoon, less for a three-squad platoon. Any supporting weapons were positioned to fire through gaps between platoons, and were to remain no more than 200 yards to the rear so that

The Soviet Union was one of very few countries to issue body armour to special assault engineers – albeit in limited quantities; here the foreground man wears the SN-42 vest, 2mm (0.8in) thick and weighing 3.5kg (7.7lb). Note that both soldiers wear camouflage coveralls, and the background man carries an ROKS-2 flamethrower.

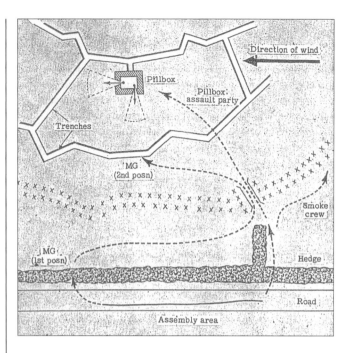

(map labels)

Direction of wind

Pillbox

Pillbox
assault party

Trenches

MG
(2nd posn)

MG
(1st posn)

Smoke
crew

Hedge

Road

Assembly area

Standard German tactics were for a pioneer obstacle-breaching troop to cut or blast their way through the wire while the smoke party (*Nebeltrupp*) manoeuvred up-wind to place smoke-pots; the latter might then assault through to the rear of the objective, to give fire support or join the assault party. The assault party (*Stosstrupp*) attacked through the gapped wire, covered by the MG party (*Deckungstrupp*) from a flank.

they could displace forward in stages to ensure continuous fire support. The platoon commander remained to the rear directing the weapons, while his deputy (platoon sergeant) led the squads into the attack. Once even part of the platoon had reached the objective the platoon commander would move forward with the weapons. In practice, it was soon found that the platoon commander had to lead from the front.

When advancing through forest one squad was pushed forward in a skirmish line about 30 yards across; two squads followed 20–50 yards behind, in column formations separated laterally by less than 100 yards; any fourth squad trailed to the rear, and the command group was in the centre of the diamond. Squad LMGs were forward; grenades and bayonets were expected to be used in close combat, and the increasing issue of short-ranged SMGs encouraged closing with the enemy as fast as possible. In the restricted visibility of forested terrain little use was made of supporting weapons, which followed well to the rear.

A company tasked to assault a fortified position was organized into clearing, assault and fire groups, and two rifle platoons. The clearing group numbered 10–15 attached sappers with bangalores, demolitions, mine probes and detectors and wire-cutters; they might be issued with armoured vests. The assault group had two rifle sections, and a sapper section (demolition charges, wire-cutters, one or two flamethrowers); the fire group had one or two heavy MGs, an AT rifle, a mortar platoon (3x 50mm), and possibly one or two 76mm regimental guns.

Precise planning was undertaken: specific routes, and positions to be attacked, when and by whom, were designated, and exact targets were assigned to the fire group. The clearing group moved out at night to cut lanes under the cover of artillery barrages, and patrols attempted to determine the extent of damage. At the appointed hour the wire was blown as the artillery again opened fire to isolate specific bunkers. The assault group plunged through the gaps, with the fire group giving close-range support. Individual bunkers were attacked with sapper flamethrowers and demolitions, while automatic weapons fired on the embrasures. If bunkers or strongpoints proved particularly difficult to crack, the supporting weapons would redouble their fire or even be reinforced. The assault squads surrounded the bunkers and then broke in; the other rifle platoons were brought through the gaps, along with supporting weapons, to mop up and prepare to face a counter-attack. Assault companies were quickly spent when attacking German strongpoints, and entire battalions would be brought up to replace them. If the terrain permitted, with AT obstacles breached and enough enemy AT guns neutralized, then tanks and large-calibre SP assault guns would join in the assault, often with eight infantrymen clinging to their decks – *tankovye desant,* 'tank-jumpers'.

Germany

The Germans typically demonstrated a great deal of flexibility and initiative in their assault tactics. They placed much reliance on supporting weapons, especially MGs, for close- and long-range domination; but, like the British, they also trained in standardized step-by-step battle drills for small-unit tactics, a concept they pioneered.

German doctrine called for minimal exposure of troops until absolutely necessary; squad and platoon leaders were to observe from concealment while the rest of their unit remained under cover. The squads' LMGs might be positioned to cover the front or an exposed flank, but most riflemen remained hidden. Emphasis was placed on detailed reconnaissance and selecting approach routes for assault groups through dead ground and other cover, to lend speed and surprise to the eventual attack.

Once favourable positions were occupied, one or two squads – the *Deckungstrupp* (covering troop) – would place suppressive fire on the enemy position, while one or two others manoeuvred from the flanks, led by the platoon leader; this *Stosstrupp* (shock troop) was often kept small to minimize casualties. A smoke troop *(Nebeltrupp)* might be employed to ignite smoke-pots, smoke-candles or grenades upwind of the objective. If a manoeuvring group was pinned down by enemy fire the others would continue; it was reasoned that in this way they would reduce the amount of fire directed at the pinned group. If the advancing group's flank was endangered, their MG would shift targets. Meanwhile, the 5cm platoon mortar fired on the target or adjacent positions, displacing to follow the platoon headquarters. Regimental infantry guns and battalion heavy MGs and mortars supported the assault, firing on adjacent positions; 2cm light Flak cannons were also found especially valuable for suppressing bunkers. The group overrunning the target cleared it while the other groups took up positions beyond it, pursued any survivors with fire, and prepared for a counter-attack. Sometimes artillery was fired not only to soften up the position, but to create sheltering craters for the attackers.

The German platoon's light machine guns – here, an MG34 – provided suppressive fire both from the *Deckungstrupp* and within the *Stosstrupp*. This LMG has been displaced from its original position on a flank, to fire from the newly gapped wire as the assault develops; it may soon move forward again to take part in the final firefight on the objective, and will then set up to fight off the expected counter-attack while the position is consolidated. (Courtesy Concorde Publications)

For particularly heavy defences and formidable obstacles a pioneer assault squad was attached to a rifle platoon. All personnel were armed with 4 to 7 grenades and rifles, except the squad leader with an SMG, and the machine-gunner and flame-gunner (who also had pistols). The squad leader additionally carried 2 smoke grenades and wire-cutters; the 2-man smoke troop carried 4 smoke grenades and 10 smoke-pots; the 2-man wire-cutting team had 2 bangalores and wire-cutters; the 3-man bunker assault troop carried 2 pole charges or other demolitions; the 2-man flamethrower team were also armed with grenades, and a few more were carried by the 3-man MG team. If the pioneer squad's MG was not employed, support being provided by the rifle platoon, then these men were held in reserve and carried ammunition.

The pioneer squad would lead the assault, with the rifle platoon providing supporting fire. The MG was set up to cover the bunker embrasures while the smoke team positioned itself upwind. The squad leader indicated where the gap was to be cut, and ordered the smoke released. The wire-cutting team would begin their breach on a blind side if possible, and avoided using bangalores unless the wire was particularly dense or contained mines. The wire-cutters would then pass through and begin clearing outlying fighting positions; the bunker assault and flamethrower teams followed them through, with the smoke troop providing covering fire. The flamethrower was turned on the embrasures (it was calculated that one fuel load would be enough); when the flame-gunner announced 'Last burst', the bunker assault party immediately thrust pole charges into the embrasures or used shaped charges to blast through shutters or doors. The pioneer squad would assemble on the far side of the bunker and prepare for a counter-attack, while the rifle platoon moved in to clear the bunker and surrounding positions.

Late in the war two LMGs were often assigned to rifle squads, which gave them more flexibility in the assault. The squad would divide into shock and covering troops; the *Stosstrupp* had a 2-man LMG crew, a rifle-grenadier, and up to 4 riflemen including the leader, all with at least 4 grenades. The 3- or 4-man *Deckungstrupp* had the task of pinning down enemy movement with its LMG plus a sharpshooter with a telescope-sighted rifle (not a qualified sniper with a 4x power telescope, but a 'designated marksman' with a 1.5x scope).

Although supported by engineers with demolitions and flamethrowers, Japanese infantry were well trained to breach obstacles themselves. In this 1930s training exercise a soldier cuts wire while covered by riflemen (for training purposes smooth rather than barbed wire was used, to save expense). It was calculated that it took one man 2–3 hours to cut silently through 6 yards of wire, and two men 1½ to 2½ hours.

When advancing in dense forest, the 1944–45 squad would be forward in line with an LMG at both ends, able to cover the front with overlapping fires as well as firing to the flanks. The other two squads would follow in columns, or in lines echeloned to the right and left, with one LMG forward and one at the tail end able to cover a flank or the rear. If engaged, the echeloned squads could move forward to come on line with the lead squad, or swing to a flank. If attacked by a superior force the echeloned squads would swing inward to form a triangular hedgehog position. In forests the range advantage of the battalion's tripod-mounted MGs could not be put to effective use, so they were deployed forward with the rifle platoons in the LMG role.

Japan

The Japanese Imperial Army was noted for speed and aggression, executing bold flanking and encircling attacks even at lower echelons; for attacking through terrain considered practically impassable; for infiltration, and night attacks. (All armies employed night attacks, but the Japanese more frequently than others.) However, regardless of doctrine, Japanese attacks suffered from certain important flaws: poor reconnaissance; piecemeal attacks; lack of co-ordination between different attacking elements and their support; and frontal attacks that were all too often suicidal, especially given their limited artillery and mortar support.

The Japanese fielded the largest infantry platoon of any army – officially, 54 men armed with three LMGs and three to six 'knee mortars' – and additional LMGs were often issued. Instead of being called 'rifle sections' the squads were designated 'light machine gun sections', emphasizing their reliance on the automatic weapons.

The enveloping attack was preferred even at platoon level. Two squads would fix the enemy position, and one would manoeuvre to a flank and attack, while the position was suppressed by LMG, 'knee mortar' and rifle fire. The enveloping movement was often made over concealed ground thought impassable by the defenders. The platoon commander would remain with the main body, the enveloping squad being led by its leader.

Although Japanese doctrine cautioned against frontal assaults, in practice they frequently launched them, due to their characteristic indoctrination to attack and annihilate the enemy by a headlong rush, counting on their warrior spirit (seishin) to counter any material superiority enjoyed by the enemy. Terrain and enemy dispositions might prevent an enveloping attack; infiltration and probes would then precede the main attack to locate weak sectors, and it was on those that the assault would fall. The goal was to penetrate deep into the enemy's rear and attack command posts, artillery and services. Tanks would be employed if available – the Japanese employed tanks almost solely for infantry support.

When time permitted, a thorough reconnaissance of the enemy position and its approaches was conducted by 4- to 6-man patrols, and observation posts were established to report new developments. The patrols were conducted at night, and might include probes to provoke the enemy into firing and revealing their positions. The distance and direction to their positions were measured from recognizable terrain features, and the types and locations of obstacles were also reported. On the night of the attack a patrol would mark the approach with white rags or paper, and post guides at difficult places. Coloured flares might be fired at designated times from a nearby hill to help moving troops remain oriented; pairs of lights might be oriented to the rear, which when aligned indicated the correct route.

The approach was made in absolute silence. Heavy weapons remained behind, to be brought up once the objective was secured to fight off any counter-attack; even the LMGs brought up the rear of each squad. The assault troops would try to infiltrate the position, and would not initiate action until the enemy opened fire or they were inside his perimeter. Diversions would often be conducted elsewhere on the line, and artillery and mortars were fired into the enemy's rear areas to distract defenders and cover any noise made by infiltrators. If light obstacles were encountered, a few men within the platoon were selected to breach them. If sturdy obstacles and pillboxes barred the way, a 15-man engineer squad would be attached at company level; bangalores and demolition charges would be emplaced silently and not blown until the attack was launched. Gaps in the wire would be cut by hand if possible; the attacking platoons crawled quietly to the cut gaps, or to within a safe distance if they were to be blown.

When the charges were blown or the troops were ordered to charge through the gaps they were supposed to do so in silence, preferably clearing the objective with bayonets. Infantry or engineer squads were detailed to attack pillboxes once the perimeter was penetrated, and others to occupy positions on the flanks to fight off counter-attacks. The main body would continue to advance through the position to its main objective, which might be enemy command posts, artillery lines or supply dumps.

* * *

However much the nature of warfare has changed since World War II, the basic principles of infantry assault tactics remain unaltered today. The three main elements of the assault – the breaching/clearing force, assault force, and covering/fire support force – remain valid; and to carry successfully a stoutly defended enemy position still requires the same degree of leadership, planning, co-ordination, skill and motivation as it did more than 60 years ago.

RECOMMENDED READING

Daugherty, Leo J. III, *Fighting Techniques of a Japanese Infantryman 1941–1945* (St Paul, MN; MBI Publishing, 2002)

Daugherty, Leo J. III, *Fighting Techniques of a US Marine 1941–1945* (St Paul, MN; MBI Publishing, 2000)

English, John A., *On Infantry* (New York; Praeger, 1981)

Farrar-Hockley, Anthony, *The Mechanics of War: Infantry Tactics 1939–1945* (Warren, MI; Almark, 1976)

Gawne, Jonathan, *Spearheading D-Day: American Special Units of the Normandy Invasion* (Paris; Histoire & Collections, 1998)

PLATE COMMENTARIES

A: GERMAN PIONEERS BREACHING BARBED WIRE, 1940–41

Here 'weiss Pionieren' of an infantry regiment (as opposed to 'black pioneers', so-called from the black *Waffenfarbe* of the Pioniertruppe on their shoulder straps), cut through an entanglement using the large issue wire-cutters. If noise was not a factor, hatchets – often issued one per infantry squad – could also be used to hack through wire secured to posts, as could entrenching tools. If they are taken under fire, or detect mines in the wire, the pioneers will shove in the steel bangalore (*Rohrladung Stahl, 3kg*) – here with two tubes coupled – and the expedient extended charge (*Gestreckteladung*), a 2m-long plank with 200g TNT charges wired on; both will be detonated with a blasting cap igniter set. To screen their activities, smoke hand grenades (*Nebelhandgranate 39B*) are being thrown.

B: US FLAMETHROWER ASSAULT TEAM, TARAWA, 1943

Knowing they were tackling an extremely well-fortified island, the 2nd Marine Division engineers organized assault platoons with three 19-man squads, the squads being broken down into three six-man assault teams and attached to rifle platoons. A team had a team leader (carbine), flamethrower operator (pistol), assistant flamethrower operator (shotgun), and three demolition men (rifles). The

The German *Sprengkörper 28* (see Plate E3) was a Bakelite-encased 200g picric acid charge. Here it is fitted with the standard blasting cap igniter set or *Sprengkapselzünder*: a Bakelite detonater-holder (*Zünderhälter*) containing a blasting cap (*Sprengkäpsel Nr.8 A1*) is screwed into its central well, and linked by time fuse (*Zeitzünderschnur*), cut to the desired length and crimped, to a *Brunnzünde BZ 29* friction pull-igniter. (Private collection)

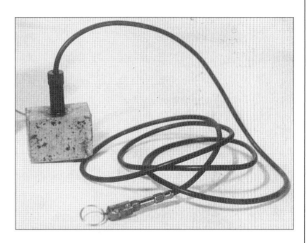

team was provided with three MC-1942 Cole handcarts loaded with two 5gal flame fuel cans, two spare hydrogen propellant tanks, 50x ½lb TNT charges, 50x 2¼lb C2 plastic charges, 2x bangalore torpedoes, 6x demolition grenades, 2x incendiary grenades, 100x blasting caps, 100ft of detcord and 50ft of time fuse. The Marines were issued M1 flamethrowers just before the operation and had little opportunity to learn their strengths and limitations, resulting in their less than effective use on Tarawa.

C: US DEMOLITION ITEMS

C1: M1 bangalore torpedo (2in diam × 5ft), with nose cap and connecting sleeve; here a length of time fuse and an M2 fuse igniter is fitted. The tube contained 8½lb of amatol with a 4in TNT booster and a cap well in each end; nine connecting collars were provided in a case of 10 torpedoes, along with nose sleeves. **C2:** 13lb M2 shaped charge (7in diam × 10½in); the stand-off collar was designed to slide down from the body when the charge was positioned. **C3:** 45lb M3 shaped charge (10in diam × 15in). **C4:** 22lb M1 chain demolition satchel charge (4½in × 9in × 12in), containing **C4a** eight detcord-linked 2¼lb tetrytol charges; **C4b** M1 tetrytol charge (2in × 2in × 11in), and **C4c** cutaway showing the two tetryl booster charges cast into the ends. If needed, individual

German assault pioneers (see Plate A) were plentifully supplied with hand grenades, sometimes carrying up to seven per man. All kinds of munitions were expended freely during the assault, so follow-on troops were supposed to bring up resupplies quickly for consolidation in case of counter-attack. (Courtesy Concorde Publications)

Flamethrowers (see Plate G) wasted a good deal of ignited fuel between the nozzle and target. One way to avoid this was to spray the target with unignited fuel, which had a longer range, and then ignite it with a short flame-burst or by firing tracers or flares at it. A drawback of this method was that it lacked the terrifying bellowing noise of burning fuel gushing through embrasures, which often persuaded bunker crews to surrender after one demonstration. Besides inflicting severe burns, the flames that penetrated an enclosed position consumed oxygen and suffocated the occupants, ignited all combustible materials and set off munitions.

blocks could be cut off leaving an 8in length of detcord attached. The M2 satchel charge was the same but the blocks were not linked by detcord. **C5:** ½lb TNT block (1in × 1in × 3in), one of the most widely used combat demolition charges. **C6:** 1lb TNT block (1in × 1in × 7in), late war issue. **C7:** 2¼lb M3 C2 PE block (2in × 2in × 11in); eight were issued in the same haversack as the M1 charges. **C8:** Can of 50 non-electric blasting caps. **C9:** Box for 10 blasting caps, as issued in dark red or natural wood. **C10:** M1 friction fuse lighter. **C11:** M2 waterproof fuse lighter, with carton for 10 lighters. **C12:** Fuse crimper (7in); the lower notch cuts safety fuse and detcord, and the upper crimps blasting caps to the cut ends. **C13:** 24in wire-cutter. **C14:** 8in M1938 wire-cutter and carrier; many wire-cutters had insulated handles to protect from electrical shock – not because electrified fences were used, but for cutting power and telephone lines. **C15:** 10-cap blasting machine (6in high).

Demolition kits were provided to engineer and often to infantry units. Typically these were canvas or leather haversacks containing such items as a crimper, wire-cutters, a knife, tape, and fuse holders (for screwing into charge wells to hold detonators in place). If electrical firing systems were used then a blasting machine (traditionally called a 'hellbox') was needed, with spools of insulated firing wire and a galvanometer for circuit-testing.

D: BRITISH & SOVIET DEMOLITION ITEMS
British:
D1: 4oz plastic explosive (PE) cartridge (1in diam × 4in). **D2:** 8oz No.2 PE cartridge (1¼in diam × 8in). **D3:** No.73 Mk I AT or 'thermos flask' grenade (3½in diam × 11 in long). **D4:** No.75 AT grenade/mine or 'Hawkins grenade' (3.7in × 6.5in). **D5:** 15lb No.3 Mk I Hayrick linear shaped charge (6in × 11½in × 17in). **D6:** No.1 Mk I shaped charge (6.1in diam × 7in). **D7:** 'Demolition set' – 1oz Mk II dry guncotton primer (1¼in long × 1.35in diam top, 1.15in diam bottom), pierced for blasting

cap crimped to length of safety fuse, the fuse pierced and a match pushed through. **D8:** Mk I folding wire-cutters. **D9:** Blasting cap crimper. **D10:** Mk I exploder dynamotor condenser – the British blasting machine.
Soviet:
D11: 75g TNT cartridge (30mm diam × 70mm). **D12:** 200g picric acid (*melinit*) block (25mm × 50mm × 100mm). **D13:** 400gm TNT block (50mm × 50mm × 100mm), showing second cap well. **D14:** 5kg TNT unitary charge. **D15:** PM-1 blasting machine; the charging handle was detachable and a door protected the firing wire connectors. **D16:** Wire-cutters.

E: GERMAN & JAPANESE DEMOLITION ITEMS
German:
E1: *Rohrladung, Stahl 3kg* bangalore (each section 1.9in diam × 3.6ft). **E2–E5:** Small bulk demolition charges – **E2** 100g *Bohrpatrone 28*, **E3** 200g *Sprengkörper 28*, **E4** 1kg *Sprengbüchse 24*, **E5** 3kg *Geballte Ladungen*, with *Sprengkapselzünder* (blasting cap, igniter and time fuse). Note that the Wehrmacht also used Czechoslovak, Polish, French, Soviet, and any other demolition materials they could lay their hands on. **E6:** 13.5kg *Hohlladung* on integral legs (13.5in diam × 10.1in). **E7:** Two-piece 50kg hollow charge (19.1in diam × 13.8in). **E8:** *Glühzündapparat 37* (electric igniter). **E9:** *Würgezange nA* (cap crimpers, new type – the old type, still in use, was similar to the US crimper). **E10:** *kleiner Drahtzange* (small wire-cutters).
Japanese:
E11: *Hakai-to* bangalore (2in diam × 46in). **E12 & E13:** 100g cylindrical, and 400g block TNT or picric acid charges. **E14:** *99 Hako-bakurai* Type 99 armour-destroying charge (4.75in diam × 1.5in deep). **E15:** 4x Type 99 charges wired between split logs. Apart from the percussion-initiated 10-second delay fuse, a length of time fuse could be inserted in a fuse well.

F: BRITISH MOUSE-HOLING CHARGE, 1944–45

In every army improvised munitions were used, and some of the successful examples were taken up officially. For instance, in Italy a British sergeant developed the 'Cross cocktail' – a 40mm Bofors AA gun cartridge case filled with guncotton and fitted with a grenade delay fuse, employed to knock out bunkers. The 'mouse-holing charge', perfected from a British Home Guard prototype in 1943 by Canadians at Ortona, was a notably successful device whose descendants are still in use today. It was a wooden frame measuring 2ft × 3ft, made of 2in × 2in or 1in × 4in lumber, and braced against a wall by a slanted plank. No.75 'Hawkins' mines or 1lb demolition changes were fastened to each corner, and sometimes to the centre for thick walls. A length of cordex with a blasting cap was inserted in each charge, linked in the centre or to the fifth charge, to which a 'demolition set' with delay fuse was attached. The recommended way to use this set was to pierce a hole through the end of the fuse and push a large-headed match through up to the head; this was ignited by rubbing it with a matchbox. When firing this powerful charge, troops had to vacate the room (and even the next room, to be safe); here a soldier of 8th Bn Royal Scots, 15th (Scottish) Div, is warning his mate, who has been covering the window, to be ready to run. Mouse-holing charges blasted man-sized openings through walls and floors to allow access into buildings, between rooms and between connected buildings; before clambering through the resultant hole the soldier would toss a grenade through. Such charges were also used to blast escape routes; if possible, assault troops avoided entering or leaving buildings through doors and windows, as these would be targeted by the enemy.

G: US ATTACK ON GERMAN BUNKER, 1944–45

Many German *Westwall* bunkers had limited fields of fire and were blind on three sides. However, the double set of heavy steel doors were located in the front and covered by the bunker's machine gun. To attack such a position the assault team stayed out of the MG34's segment of fire, suppressing fire from the embrasure with automatic weapons and bazookas. Smoke might be used to blind the bunker crew, as the M2-2 flamethrower and 2.36in M9A1 bazooka teams closed in. Flame bursts and bazooka rockets might not knock out the compartmentalized bunkers, but they would drive the defenders away from embrasures to allow satchel changes to be flung in.

Flamethrowers were hated by the intended victims, who targeted the burdened, slow-moving flame-gunners (although, contrary to Hollywood wisdom, the detonation of fuel tanks was very rare). There were also many grisly stories about the fate of captured flame-gunners.

H: SOVIET ATTACK ON GERMAN TWO-MAN STEEL PILLBOX

The Red Army found the German 4-ton portable steel pillbox (*fahrbare Panzerlafette,* 'transportable armour mount', or *gepanzerte Krabbe,* 'armoured crab') troublesome. A two-man shelter mounting an MG42 with a 60-degree arc of fire, it was easy to dig in and camouflage, proof against most infantry weapons, and was installed in mutually supporting

clusters. In the absence of point-blank tank or artillery fire support, the Soviets made do with what they had. If artillery or mortar fire happened to blow away the earth cover, 14.5mm AT rifles could penetrate the lower side and rear armour, but this would seldom happen. The periscope could be smashed by rifle fire, reducing visibility to the peephole in the MG embrasure; and if infantry could avoid supporting fires and get up close, it might be possible to cover up the peephole with earth. The ventilation flue was vulnerable to Molotov cocktails, and the armour to satchel charges and AT grenades – such as the illustrated Soviet RPG-40 and captured German *Haft-Hohlladung 3kg* magnetic mine. The rear hatch opened outwards, so might be jammed shut with rocks or logs to trap the crew. Here the SMG gunner is about to persuade the occupants to close the hatch, so he and his comrade can apply the magnetic hollow charge, without interference, to what is about to become a steel tomb.

Known as the 'armour-cracker' *(Panzerknacker)*, the *Haft-Hohlladung 3kg* (see Plate H) measured 6.5in in diameter by 10in high. Such shaped charges were filled with a high-speed explosive, usually pentolite (TNT and PETN) cast with a cone-shaped cavity lined with thin metal. The charge was placed separated from the target surface by a short 'stand-off' distance. When it was detonated, the metal lining formed a molten 'slug' which punched a narrow tunnel through the material at approximately 33,000ft per second, carrying with it fragments from both the projectile and the material. This penetrated armour two or three times the diameter of the cone, and a considerably thicker layer of reinforced concrete. (Private collection)

INDEX

Figures in **bold** refer to illustrations.